Contents

Introduction

The subjects of this book are the suffering children of the world who are mostly nameless and whose voices are not heard. The count of these children is in the millions. Whether the AIDS orphans and the starving children of Africa, the child labourers in India, the child soldiers in Afghanistan or the victims of drug and alcohol abuse in the UK, throughout the world, in every nation, vast numbers of children are suffering from the moment they are born.

It has been said that a civilised society is judged by the way it treats its children. On this count alone we, as citizens of the UK, stand condemned by the evidence of neglect and abuse set out in this book. In this age of global communication, trade and partnerships, however, it could be reasonably asserted that a generation can be judged by the way it treats not just its own children, but the children of the whole world.

In 1993 the Maranatha Community made 'A Call to the Nation'. This document, launched in the Houses of Parliament, pointed to the evidence of decline and disintegration in our national life. We identified children as the cause for greatest concern and subsequently published 'What on Earth are we doing to our Children? - an appeal to the Nation's conscience' in March 1995. This was presented at a meeting in the House of Lords, chaired by Viscount Caldecott, who referred to it as "A document of crucial importance today". The book, now in its 10th edition, was subsequently debated in the House of Commons and was the subject of a consultation in the House of Lords, opened by the Lord Chancellor. Following this, Andrew Rowe MP, took the initiative of convening a group of those concerned for children to lead a national conference at Coventry Cathedral entitled 'Heirs to the Millennium' at which children made a significant contribution.

The publication 'What on Earth are we doing to our Children?' presented devastating information about the suffering of children throughout the world, but particularly in the United Kingdom. It served as a catalyst, prompting many to take action on behalf of children. Significantly, this was before the internet or mobile phones were widely available.

In 1998 The Maranatha Community convened the first national conference on child abuse, bringing together a large number of participants from the police, immigration, probation, politics, medicine, social work, the churches, victims groups and concerned individuals. Members of the Community continue to be involved in all kinds of work on behalf of children.

This publication suggests that the situation for the children and young people of the UK has become worse, not better, since the first book was written. In 2007 UNICEF ranked Britain bottom out of 21 developed countries for child welfare and third from bottom for educational standards. Other reports have labelled British children as the 'unhappiest in the world'.

Children learn their core values from the adults around them. Adults have a responsibility to teach and encourage children to develop to their full potential in every aspect of life. There are deeply worrying trends in our society which are affecting the principal values that our children are learning. Of concern to many is the escalation of materialism, an obsession with fame and notoriety, increasing family breakdown and a greater sense of children being isolated from our communities. Children are learning how to behave, relate and respond through sources that are morally corrupt yet, as adults, we are continuing to allow this to happen.

The purpose of this book is to warn of the increasingly perilous future for the children of Britain. They must be placed at the top of our political agenda. Edmund Burke wrote (1790) *"The state ... is ... a partnership not only between those who are living, but between those who are living, those who are dead, and those who are to be born."* Economists are now pointing to the huge debt that the current adult generation is bequeathing to the generations to come, rightly calling it 'intergenerational theft'. This book points to the more serious consequences of the choices made by our British society and political decision-makers over the last half century. Children today are suffering from the lack of investment in them as individual, unique human beings. The evidence points to vast numbers being without any sense of identity or purpose. What on earth have we done? What on earth are we doing to our children?

Dr. Linda Stalley
Co-Leader, Maranatha Community

A Portrait

Danny (not his real name) was around 7 years old when the first 'What on Earth are we doing to our Children?' was written. He was a much longed for child, born to a couple who wanted to complete their picture perfect life; a gorgeous baby to accessorise the designer lifestyle they were living. From the age of 3 months old Danny spent his days with child-minders and in nurseries. His parents said they wanted to give him everything they never had: designer clothes, foreign holidays and all the latest toys. What Danny needed was his parents' time. Weekends and school holidays were spent with various grandparents as his parents needed time to 'wind down and have a night out'.

When Danny was still very young his parents split in what became a bitter divorce and Danny became a weapon to be used against the other parent. While he was still in primary school he became a 'latch key kid' as his father bowed out of much of his responsibilities in order to punish his ex. As Danny became scared and lonely, fearing time alone in the house, he roamed the streets with his friends. One time, while his parents were at work, a man tried to force him into a car. Danny was frightened but his situation did not change.

From his teens he started drinking, dabbling in drugs and bringing his girlfriend home to stay over-night. His parents' response? 'I'd rather him do it here than hide it from us'. Danny had already seen a multitude of his parents' partners come and go. Both his parents were incapable of being single and various step-parents ensued. Danny saw men come and go, stepfathers who abused him and his mother, in addition to his own father who was ineffective, bitter and selfish.

By the age of 16 years it had become clear that neither of his parents wanted him at home. The reason? Their current partners didn't want children so Danny was found a flat and left alone. Without guidance and restrictions Danny did as he pleased, girls came and went, he drank, took drugs and partied. During a short relationship lasting no more than a few weeks Danny got a girl pregnant. At this point he was also involved with another girl. Within weeks she was pregnant too. That baby was miscarried, the next was aborted and the third was born roughly a year after the first. Before the age of 20 years he had two children by two different teenage girls. Danny's justification? 'I'm just the same as all my mates'. When that relationship ended in heartbreak, violence and despair Danny was alone again.

Strings of women followed. He lost his job, his driving licence to a drink driving conviction and was caught by the police carrying drugs. These convictions were added to the catalogue of minor convictions he had received in the past for drugs and fighting. The life he is leading isn't that different to that of his peers. Sadly, Danny is the rule rather than the exception. Today he is 22 years old. He is still living in the tangled mess that is his life, seeing his kids at the weekends, lurching from one 'relationship' to another and living without hope, believing that this is all life has to offer.

1   Denied the Right to Live

- Worldwide, about 29,000 children under the age of five - 21 each minute - die every day, mainly from preventable causes. *(UNICEF, 2011)*

- There are an estimated 250 million underweight children in the world and 20% of children in developing countries are moderately or severely underweight. *(Asian Scientist, July 2012)*

- In the last decade 2,000,000 children have been killed and 6,000,000 permanently disabled or seriously injured during armed conflict. *(Religious Tolerance, 2010)*

- On average, every week in England and Wales, one child is killed at the hands of another person. Almost two thirds of children killed are under five years of age. Every ten days one child is killed at the hands of their parent. *(NSPCC, 2011)*

- Since 1990 82 children have been executed worldwide. *(Amnesty International, 2009)*

The wealth of the nations is unequally balanced with poorer countries continuing in the downward spiral of poverty and despair. We spend more on leisure and pleasure than on the starving children of the world.

4,000 children are dying each day from diarrhoea caused by dirty water and lack of sanitation. *(UNICEF, 27 October 2010)*

A 20 cigarette per day habit in the UK will cost a smoker well over £2000 each year yet just £15 is enough to help one person gain access to safe water, sanitation and hygiene education. *(Water Aid, 2011)*

Britain fights an epidemic of obesity. Worldwide, in 2007, there were 146 million underweight children. 70% of these children were living in just 10 countries. 6.54 million children under five were dying each year from malnutrition and hunger related diseases. *(UNICEF, 2007)*

The investment houses' decision to move into speculation in the commodity prices of food has had tragic consequences for children of the world as world food prices have risen steeply. This has led to riots, famine and many deaths. Food prices across the world have started to soar with rice alone increasing 320%. Worldwide, 200 million people, mostly children, who relied on these cheaply imported foodstuffs have descended into malnutrition or starvation. *(Daily Mail, 20 July 2010)*

The global food supplement industry is worth £16.5 billion each year *(The Guardian, 8 February 2009)*. Yet 640,000 child deaths could be prevented annually by increasing access to vitamin A and zinc. *(WFP Annual Report, 2007)*

When a society starts to kill children something is very wrong. The right to life is fundamental, yet millions of children are being denied this right for many distasteful and perplexing reasons.

There are an estimated 250,000 child soldiers in the world today. *(War Child, 2010)*

Children are regularly used as soldiers. They are easier to condition and brainwash, don't need to be paid as much or need as much food. They are also less aware of the risks they are taking, which makes them a lot easier to send into the line of fire. As they are small and considered an expendable commodity they are often sent into battle as scouts or decoys in order to draw the enemy's fire. *(War Child, 2010)*

Children were actively involved in armed conflict in government forces or non-state armed groups in 19 countries or territories between April 2004 and October 2007. The tasks they carry out include direct combat, laying mines and explosives, scouting, spying, acting as decoys, domestic labour and even sexual slavery. *(Child Soldiers, 2008)*

In Afghanistan the Taliban use children to plant bombs, run weapons and carry out daily tasks for them. This is because they know the British Army won't fire on children. A fifth of roadside bombs have been set by children. This has led to the death and injury of the children used. Children have also been deployed as suicide bombers. *(Daily Telegraph, 30 June 2010)*

2   Deprived of a Family

- Nearly a quarter (24%) of children live with only one parent and nine out of 10 of those households were headed by lone mothers *(The Office for National Statistics, 2012)*

- More children are born in Britain today outside of marriage than in most other European countries. The average figure in 2007 was 44%, compared with just 3% in Cyprus, and just 12% in Britain in the early 1970s. *(BBC, 2007)* By 2010 the number of children in England and Wales born outside marriage had reached 338,790, just under half of the 723,165 babies born that year. *(The Office for National Statistics, quoted in The Daily Mail, 11th April 2012)*

- A third of children fail to stay in touch with one of their parents following a divorce. *(The Times, 16 November 2009)*

- Forty eight percent of all children born today will experience the breakdown of their parents' relationship. *(Centre for Social Justice, May 2012)*

- Forty five percent of marriages end in divorce. *(The Office for National Statistics, 2008)*

- It is estimated that approximately 200,000 children had a parent in prison at some point in 2009. *(Ministry of Justice, 2012)*

The face of the 'family' has changed in recent decades. The Office for National Statistics *(2007)* has said children in the UK were three times more likely to live in one-parent households than they were in 1972, with the number of lone parent families reaching almost two million for the first time. *(The Office of National Statistics, 2012)* Yet evidence shows that children raised within a traditional family fare best in life.

In 1990, 75% of children lived with both their mother and father. Over the next two decades this dropped to 60%. Children from broken homes are very vulnerable. The London University's Institute of Education said that children of separated parents are *'at significantly greater risk than those whose parents remain together'*. *(Daily Mail, 13 October 2009)*

The basic concept of family life has been challenged to the extent that it is no longer considered the norm for children to be raised with a mother and father in one home. Parents and siblings have become as interchangeable as addresses. There is evidence that children whose parents split up are three times more likely to become aggressive or badly behaved. Living in a "blended" family containing step-children or step-parents increases the risk of developing behavioural problems still further. *(Office for National Statistics, 2008)*

Though it has been argued that children do not suffer significantly when their parents split up the short and long term effects on the child cannot be underestimated: *'children in single-parent and co-habiting families are more likely to suffer physical abuse, to fail at school, play truant, suffer from depression and other mental illnesses or turn to drugs and alcohol. The rising level of social dysfunction mirrors a rising level of family fragmentation... if the family fails, society breaks up - and there are many signs of this happening'*. *(Centre for Policy Studies, April 2009)*

Schools are increasingly carrying the burden of family breakdown in Britain. Some children arrive at school without basic life skills. They are unable to use a knife and fork, sit at a table or engage in conversation. For many pupils school has become the sole constant in their chaotic lives, the only place they experience clear moral boundaries. *(Daily Telegraph, 10 March 2008)*

The lack of support for the marriage-based family by successive governments has taken its toll. The UK has developed a state benefit system which appears to encourage lone parenting whilst penalising two parent families. A two parent, one income, family is just over £1 per head better off than a lone parent family dependent on the state. Parents who split can increase their income by up to 65% with state benefits.

The Relationships Foundation *(4 February 2012)*, which has formulated an index to calculate the cost of family breakdown, found that in 2012 the total cost of family breakdown in the UK was almost £44 billion, an increase of £2 billion since 2011. The annual cost of this to each taxpayer is now £1,470.

However, the financial cost of marriage breakdown is insignificant compared to the mental, emotional and spiritual cost to thousands of children who suffer pain, rejection, insecurity and confusion. Victims of marriage breakdown often associate marriage and family with pain and so they more readily reject marriage as an option, thus continuing the cycle.

Family breakdown is linked to anti-social behaviour. *'We know that the majority of young offenders come from broken homes, nearly two thirds have drug and alcohol addiction problems, more than three in four have no educational qualifications and many young prisoners have mental health problems rooted in drug abuse...Broken families, however, are often the places where the seeds are sown for future criminal activity'. (Centre for Social Justice, 2007)*

The skills for raising children have been eroded as we now have children or poorly-parented adults raising the next generation. As a result children are searching elsewhere for acceptance and belonging, leading to more and more children becoming involved in gangs and criminal activity.

Advances in science have blurred the lines of parenthood and family. Laws made to keep pace with this ever-advancing technology have made it possible for as many as five adults to be involved in the procurement of a child: egg donor, sperm donor, surrogate mother and adoptive parents, thus creating a history so complicated no one is able to decide accurately who is the actual parent of the child. This leads to confusion when children try to identify their family background – who are they?

Artificial conception techniques have moved our society towards regarding the conception of children as a commodity. It has become a right, rather than a privilege, to have a child and the family situation they are born into becomes a secondary consideration. These so called advances have opened the door to 'alternative' families where the rights of the parents are valued much more highly than those of the child. A child's right to both a father and mother is no longer considered. Rather, the ideal of a man and woman marrying to create a family is presented as old fashioned, out-dated and oppressive.

The Gay Liberation Front manifesto states: *'The oppression of gay people starts in the most basic unit of society, the family, consisting of the man in charge, a slave as his wife, and their children on whom they force themselves as the ideal models. The very form of the family works against homosexuality'*. The manifesto further declares: **'We must aim at the abolition of the family'**. *(Gay Liberation Front, 1979)*

Despite this view the marriage based family is still the bedrock of a stable and constructive society. *'Marriage is not just a piece of paper (only 9% of people in the 2001-2 British Social Attitudes survey thought that it was, whereas 59% said it was the best kind of relationship). Its significance lies in the fact that it provides a meaningful and beneficial life script, a map of life that helps young people to plan, to be self-disciplined, to defer gratification. Success in today's knowledge economy depends upon these character qualities as never before. When marriage became optional, disadvantaged communities lost one of their few institutional supports for planning ahead and taking control of their lives'*. *(Centre for Social Justice, 2007)*

The family should be a place where children are nurtured, learn and grow. It is a place to develop a clear understanding of what a healthy human relationship is and a lifelong moral framework. The newly accepted practice of rejecting the traditional Christian family and embracing a variety of humanist alternatives has shown itself to be disastrous. The human suffering resulting from this is immense.

3   Denied the right to be Born

- 43,800,000 children were aborted worldwide in 2008. *(Guttmacher Institute 2012)*

- In Europe 30% of pregnancies end in abortion. *(Guttmacher Institute 2012)*

- There is an abortion every 11 seconds in Europe equating to 2.9 million every year. *(Institute for Family Policies, 2010)*

- In England and Wales nearly half of conceptions in girls under the age of 18 ended in abortion. *(Office for National Statistics, 2008)*

- Between 2000 and 2007 a total of 15 girls aged 10 and 39 girls aged 11 have become pregnant. *(Daily Telegraph, 8 February 2010)*

- The Department of Health's abortion statistics report that in 2010 there were 189,574 abortions in England and Wales. *(NHS News, 14 May 2012)*

The destruction of children in the womb has become a well-established, worldwide practice. This is despite the fact that nearly half of all abortions worldwide are considered unsafe. There are 31 abortions for every 100 live births worldwide and this ratio is the highest in Eastern Europe with 105 abortions for every 100 live births. *(The Lancet, 2007)*

In England and Wales 22% of conceptions ended in abortion *(Office for National Statistics, 2008)* with 94% of abortions being funded by the NHS. *(Department of Health, 2009)*

Abortion has become an ever more profitable activity with 2010 seeing the UK's first screening on TV of an advertisement for a leading abortion provider. While some abortion charities maintain that they make no profit the simple fact is unless they carry out abortions they do not get paid. *(The Guardian, 19 May 2010)*

For the first time in history women have had effective control over their ability to reproduce. Remarkably the trend for repeat abortions has not diminished and abortion is increasingly being used as a method of contraception.

Figures from 2009 showed that the proportion of all abortions that are considered repeat abortions has increased from 30% to 34% since 2000. *(NHS News, 14th May 2012)* More than 1000 women or girls underwent at least their fifth termination, including 214 on their sixth, 70 on their seventh and 48 who underwent the procedure for at least the eighth time. *(Department of Health, 2009)*

The current UK abortion deadline is 24 weeks gestation. With the advancing capability of medical science more and more babies are surviving being delivered before this cut off point. The Confidential Inquiry into Maternal and Child Health *(2008)* found that these late abortions have led to as many as 66 babies a year being born alive. We have a dilemma of the contradiction of a baby being delivered prematurely, at 22 weeks, receiving maximum life support in one hospital room whilst in the same hospital babies of a similar gestation are aborted and dying.

One of the largest studies of its type found that women who have undergone an abortion experienced an 81% increased risk of mental health issues. Their results revealed *'a moderate to highly increased risk of mental health problems after abortion'. (The British Journal of Psychiatry 2011, 199:180-186)*

There is also mounting evidence that the unborn child feels pain and has a memory operating from a very early stage.

Large-scale termination of pregnancy is unnatural. The womb should be a place of safety, security and nurture. It has become one of the most dangerous places for a child to be. The consequence is a significant reduction in the UK birth rate and serious questions about how a diminished future work force can sustain a longer-living, larger elderly population.

4 Deprived of Opportunity

- Worldwide 218 million children (one in seven) are working. 14% of all children aged 5-17 years are child labourers. *(Stop Child Labour, 30 March 2011)*

- In sub-Saharan Africa around one in three children are engaged in child labour, representing 69 million children. *(UNICEF, February 2011)*

- Every year 22,000 children die in work-related accidents. *(International Labour Organization, 2005)*

- The number of 16-24 year olds not in education, employment or training (NEETs) in England has reached 938,000. This represents 15.6% of this age group. *(Department for Education, 2011)*

- The cost of youth unemployment and inactivity in the UK is £155 million per week. *(The Prince's Trust, 28 March 2011)*

Across the world children are being deprived of education that would enable them to develop their natural potential. Most often this is due to the exploitation of children for cheap labour. However in the UK increasing numbers of children and young people are suffering through educational failure.

The greatest abuse of a child's right to dignity is that of poverty. Growing up in poverty has a profound impact upon children's health, education, aspirations and well-being, limiting the extent to which they can realise their full potential and often trapping them in a lifelong cycle of disadvantage and inequity. *(UNICEF, 2011)*

Children living in the poorest homes and in rural areas are most likely to be child labourers. They are working in mines, working with chemicals and pesticides or working with dangerous machinery. Child labour hinders a child's education denying them a way to escape their horrendous situation and build a better future. *(UNICEF, 30 March 2011)*

Today, throughout the world, around 215 million children work, many full-time. They are denied the chance to be children. More than half of them are exposed to the worst forms of child labour such as work in hazardous environments, slavery, or other forms of forced labour, illicit activities including drug trafficking and prostitution, as well as involvement in armed conflict. *(International Labour Organisation, 13 April 2011)*

Child labourers are cheaper and more malleable than adults. They are much more suited to certain types of work. For example in carpet making their small hands are highly sought after by manufacturers. Child workers have a limited working life. As they get older and their health deteriorates, often because of the long hours spent working in terrible conditions, they are then replaced by younger children. *(BBC World Service, Children of Conflict, 2011)*

India has one of the highest rates of child labour in the world. Children are literally sold for labour for between £5 and £20. *(Save the Children Movement, 13 April 2011)*

In the USA more than 230,000 children work in agriculture and 13,000 in sweatshops. There are 2.5 million working children in the developed economies and another 2.5 million in transition economies. *(International Labour Organisation, 2005)*

The UK is also guilty of exploiting children in the market place. Romanian children as young as nine were found working in freezing cold fields in Worcestershire. *(BBC News, October 2010)*

The British arm of international child protection charity ECPAT found that 215 children from 33 different countries were officially identified as having been trafficked into the UK between April 2009 and June 2010. The children were mostly involved in restaurant and building site labour but were also forced to work as domestic servants and on cannabis farms. *(BBC News, 25 October 2010)* This is likely to be much lower than the actual number of children involved.

The UK's secondary education standards are falling despite an investment of £30 billion. We are facing continual problems in meeting the educational needs of our children. The Programme for International Student Assessment *(PISA, 2011)* survey showed that the UK's educational results have fallen. Out of 70 countries the UK had dropped to 25th place in reading. Three years ago we came 17th. We are now on a par with Hungary and below Japan, USA, France and Germany.

One in four 11 year olds is leaving primary school without a proper grasp of the 3 Rs. The government league tables show that 112,600 pupils failed to reach the minimum standard in English and maths. *(Department of Education, December 2010)*

Britain has become the NEET capital of Western Europe. Almost one in five 18 year old boys and one in six girls qualifies as a NEET. The Department for Work and Pensions (2011) found that there are 1.5 million people in Britain who have never worked a day in their lives. Of these 600,000 were under the age of 25.

Research from The Prince's Trust (2010) suggests that *'young people who are NEET are less happy and confident in all aspects of life than those in work, education or training...A significant number regularly feel isolated, unloved, down and depressed. NEETs are more than twice as likely to feel they have nothing to look forward to in life. They also feel less valued by the people around them and are twice as likely to claim they have lost their way in life'*. Additionally, 35% of NEETs have felt suicidal. The sense of hopelessness of this lost generation is very real.

The cost of youth unemployment goes beyond the financial and becomes a major social issue with NEETs more likely to resort to crime through frustration, boredom and poverty. *'The rise in the NEET figures puts the community more at risk from crime by disaffected young people. Without the focus of a job, education or training, teenagers are more likely to turn to petty offending. They are also more at risk of falling prey to the false glamour of gang, drug and weapons related crime'*. *(NACRO, 28 August 2009)*

The statistics suggest that throughout the world children and young people are not valued or cared for as they should be. In the UK we now have a gross population imbalance. As the 'baby boomers' of the post war years start to draw pensions, we are faced with the reality of our lack of investment in the workforce of the next generation which is far smaller in number.

5 Robbed of innocence

- Nearly nine out of 10 parents surveyed for the Bailey Review agreed with the statement that 'these days children are under pressure to grow up too quickly'. *(TNS Omnibus survey, 2011)*

- 70% of teenagers have viewed online pornography *(The Henry J. Kaiser Family Foundation, 2012)*

- Nine in ten (91%) children aged 5-15 live in a household with computer internet access. *(Ofcom, 2011)*

- Forty three per cent of 12-15s have computer internet access in their bedroom. *(Ofcom, 2011)*

The pressure on children to grow up takes two different but related forms: the pressure to take part in a sexualised life before they are ready to do so; and the commercial pressure to consume the vast range of goods and services that are available to children and young people of all ages. *(Letting Children be Children, DfE, 2011)*

'The world is saturated by more images today than at any other time in our modern history. Behind each of these images lies a message about expectation, values and ideals. Women are revered – and rewarded – for their physical attributes and both boys and girls are under pressure to emulate polarised gender stereotypes from a younger and younger age'. (Papadopoulos L., Sexualisation of Young People, February 2010)

Sexual media can encourage girls and young women to see themselves primarily in sexual terms and to equate their worth and appeal within an extremely narrow standard of physical attractiveness. It also teaches young women that they only have value as an object of sexual interest. Their self-image then becomes increasingly sexualised as they measure themselves against distorted portrayals of beauty and desirability. *(American Psychological Association, 2007)*
"When I was eleven I read a teenage magazine for the first time and

that's when it kind of clicked 'I should be like this'". (Mental Health Foundation, 2008).

Celebrity worship is endemic in today's society. The role models of children today are media-hungry, fame-addicted celebrities who are valued for their sex appeal and given column inches in proportion to how badly they behave. The plastic surgery industry has exploded with younger and younger people using surgery in the pursuit of the 'ideal' body.

The social pressures on our young are significant. The eating disorder charity BEAT has estimated that there are 1.6 million people in the UK with eating disorders with children showing symptoms as young as six.

Disturbingly, young people are reporting that they get much of their sex and relationships education from pornography. This is primarily via the internet where it is mostly uncensored and unrestricted. Internet access is no longer restricted to a computer. Mobile phones and other multimedia devices provide constant, and often unmonitored, access to the internet. *(Family Planning Association, 3 May 2011)*

Sexual abuse is now recognised as being all too common in our society today. While most people associate sexual abuse with incest and child molestation there are other more subtle unrecognised forms which have very negative and long term psychological effects. The exposure of children to pornography and adult sexual behaviour is also abuse. *(California State University, 28 March 2011)*

Most internet porn is viewed unintentionally. 38% of children have seen a pornographic pop-up advert whilst doing something else; 36% have accidentally found themselves on a porn site when looking for something else; 25% have received pornographic junk mail. One third of 9-19 year old internet users have received unwanted sexual comments online or by text message. Only 7% of parents are aware that their child has received sexual comments online. *(UK Children Go Online Project, 2005)*

Dr William Struthers, (Associate Professor of Psychology, Wheaton College) told a meeting in the House of Commons that 12-18 year olds in the US and UK were "rampantly" accessing internet pornography and that teenagers are frequently emailing sexually explicit material to each other. This behaviour is not restricted to boys. Dr Struthers stated that 67% of men and 49% of women see pornography as an acceptable outlet for sexuality. *(Christianity Today, 24 May 2012)*

The sexualisation of our children is promoted by marketers using sexual imagery for children's products. Playboy bunny logos appear on children's stationery; padded bras, thongs and high heeled shoes are being sold for children as young as eight. *'Such blurring suggests that it is acceptable to impose adult sexual themes onto children, and potentially relate to children as sexual objects'. (Papadopoulos L. Sexualisation of Young People, February 2010)*

Pornography encourages sexual activity without responsibility. It encourages children to become sexually active at a younger age, thus endangering their health. Teen pregnancy rates are soaring and sexually transmitted infections are at an all-time high. Children have to carry the consequences of our neglect with them throughout their lives. *(ProtectKids.com, 28 March 2011)*

The consequences of the use of pornography are now being seen in the behaviour of young children.

In a study of Canadian teenagers, with an average age of 14, there was a strong link between boys who frequently used pornography and their agreement with the idea that it is acceptable to hold a girl down and force her to have sex. Exposure to pornography may also increase a child's own vulnerability to sexual abuse and exploitation. Some adult perpetrators use pornography as a calculated tactic to undermine children's abilities to evade or escape sexual abuse. Pornography *'shows sex in unrealistic ways and neglects intimacy and romance; most pornography is sexist; and some is based on and eroticises violence'. (Child Abuse Review Vol. 18: 384-400, 2009)*

A boy of 12 has pleaded guilty to raping a nine year old girl after watching hard core pornography online. His own lawyer warned that there is a generation of children growing up with a 'skewed view' on sex. The boy told the police he raped the girl because he wanted to 'feel grown up' after watching pornography online. He had previously had unrestricted access to the web and was able to look freely at sexually explicit material. *(Daily Mail, 31 May 2012)*

Parents are beginning to complain that school is the place that children are first exposed to indecent images. A head teacher of a school in Cornwall asked a social networking site to remove the school's profile after complaints that children as young as 13 years had put soft porn pictures of themselves on it. *(The Guardian, 30 January 2007)*

Sex education for our children is becoming more liberal and being introduced at a younger age. Children are being taught with an 'anything goes' attitude. This failing is seriously damaging our young. Local councils are using explicit books that discuss sex in blunt and adult terms to children as young as five. *The Primary School Sex And Relationships Education Pack* (HIT UK) includes material for children aged 5-11 to learn about different sexual positions and prostitution.

Despite millions of pounds being spent on sex education by successive governments teen pregnancy is increasing and sexually transmitted infections (STIs) are increasing, with one in ten young people catching a second STI within a year of a first diagnosis. *(Health Protection Agency, 2010)*

'Early sexual activity and multiple partners are also associated with pain and suffering from broken relationships, a sense of betrayal and abandonment, confusion about romantic feelings, altered self-esteem, depression, and impaired ability to form healthy long-term relationships'. (Malhotra S, *Impact of the Sexual Revolution. Journal of American Physicians and Surgeons 2008, 13: (3),82-87)*

To rob our children of their innocence, to force them to grow up before their time and to make them vulnerable to the evils in society is surely one of the greatest crimes we can commit. Is this the legacy we want to leave behind? Several recent reports have identified these dangerous trends and have made recommendations to government. It is vital that these are carried through.

6   Poisoned by an adult world

- Over the past 10 years there has been a 67% increase in the number of children born addicted to drugs in the UK with one in 500 babies needing treatment for withdrawal. *(British Association of Perinatal Medicine, 2009)*

- 15% of children in England report being regular smokers. *(Cancer Research UK, 2011)*

- The estimated cost of hospital treatment for underage drinkers in England is thought to be about £19m a year. *(Alcohol Concern, 2010)*

Children in the womb and new born babies are among the most vulnerable in society. Increasing numbers of children are being exposed to a chemical cosh and environmental pollution from as early as their day of conception. We have become a chemically dependent and careless society and children are now bearing the physical and mental scars that our adult world has inflicted upon them.

Babies born to mothers addicted to drugs or alcohol can suffer severe withdrawal symptoms, including breathing problems and convulsions and are more prone to sudden infant death syndrome. These distressing symptoms can last many weeks and exposure to drugs in the womb can lead to serious health problems in later life.

In just one year a total of 350 babies were born to addicted mothers in Manchester, Fife and Bradford alone. The increase in withdrawing babies is a reflection of the number of women abusing drugs and alcohol. Professor David Field, president of the British Association of Perinatal Medicine, said: *"In the mid-1990s, you rarely saw these babies but now there is always one on the ward who is withdrawing, and the numbers will grow as the rates of addiction continue to grow. Most women we see tend to be on heroin or methadone or both".* *(Addiction Today, June 2009)*

The long term health implications and risk of addiction and premature death from drinking at an early age are serious.

Alcohol Concern states that alcohol contributes to 5% of deaths in young people, 1.4% more than in the adult population. They go on to say it is *'a significant problem for the UK'*. The UK also has the highest rates of teenage alcohol-related injuries in Europe. Underage drinkers drink approximately the equivalent of 6.9 million pints of beer or 1.7 million bottles of wine each week with an estimated 630,000 11-17 year olds drinking twice or more per week. *(Right Time, Right Place, 2010)*

A three year old child has become the youngest person in Britain to be admitted to hospital to be treated for alcohol addiction. The child was given alcohol regularly for at least six months before admission to hospital, creating a dependency. This child was one of 13 young children who were diagnosed as alcoholic by the Heart of England NHS Trust between 2008 and 2010. In the same period 106 teenagers aged 13-16 years were also treated for their addiction to alcohol.
(The Independent, 14 March 2011)

'Binge drinking' has become habitual for many young people in Britain. 21% of pupils interviewed in England aged 11 to 15 years reported drinking alcohol in the week prior to interview with 56% of them claiming to have drunk alcohol at some point in the past. The average weekly intake of alcohol of these children was around 11.4 units. *(Statistics on Alcohol (NHS), 2007)*

Smoking remains one of the biggest killers in the UK today. The effects of smoking and the carcinogenic risk are well known. Children are still being exposed to smoking not just from adults but are smoking themselves.

Smoking in pregnancy is a major problem. The effects of exposure to cigarettes upon the child in the womb are well known and include low birth weight, prematurity, increased risk of miscarriage, still birth and cot death. The effects can last a lifetime with children being at increased risk of infections, asthma and chest infections. The NHS now provides midwives dedicated to smoking cessation. *(Smoke free NHS, 15 June 2011)*

Children as young as ten have been offered shopping vouchers to quit smoking – children too young legally to buy a pack of cigarettes. *(NHS Brighton and Hove Trust, 2009)*

Cancer Research found that 6% of children aged 11-15 years smoked at least one cigarette each week. By the age of 15 years 15% of children in England report being regular smokers despite the fact that it is illegal to sell any tobacco product to anyone under 18. There is also evidence that a younger age of smoking initiation increases the risk of lung cancer regardless of the amount smoked or how long they smoked for. *(Cancer Research, 15 June 2011)*

The undeveloped bodies and brains of children are most at risk from industrial chemicals and other unregulated pollutants. Philippe Grandjean, visiting professor at Harvard said: *"The human brain is a precious and vulnerable organ. Even limited damage may have serious consequences. It probably is going to be difficult [to set exposure limits] but this is a classical case where there really is a lot at stake. We are talking about the brain development of future generations. There will be an enormous cost of not regulating exposure". (The Independent, 8 November 2006)*

Smoking, alcohol and drugs continue to scar our national life. Social and media pressures encourage children to emulate what they see. The pursuit of profit has left very little room for conscience, leaving our children exposed and vulnerable to a toxic environment.

7   Poisoned minds by what they see

- 66% of parents in the UK think that children are able to see inappropriate content before the watershed hour and 80% of parents thought video games and films, easily accessible to children, featured too many violent or sexual themes. *(Mothers' Union, 2010)*

- 14% of 9-16 year olds have seen sexual images on websites. This included 8% of 11-16 year olds who saw images of people having sex and/or genitals, and 2% who saw violent sexual images.

- 32% of all 9-16 year olds who had seen sexual images said they were upset by them. *EU Kids Online, 2012*

- 60% of people believed that young people's self-esteem is damaged by the media's negative coverage of their age group and 69% agree that violent video games make children more aggressive. *(The Children's Society, 2008)*

It is estimated that around a third of 8-11 year olds have watched at least one adult movie. The National Viewers and Listeners Association estimate that children watch more than 1,000 shootings on television each year. *(Times Educational Supplement online, 1 July 2011)*

"If you came and you found a strange man... teaching your kids to punch each other, or trying to sell them all kinds of products, you'd kick him right out of the house, but here you are; you come in and the TV is on, and you don't think twice about it". (Jerome Singer, Yale Psychology Faculty, 16 June 2011)

Traditionally children were socialized by parents, peers, religious and educational institutions. However many studies have shown the media, especially television, is playing an increasingly important role in the socialization of our children today. *(Media and Communication Studies 2010, 2: (6),138-143)*

By the time the average American child reaches 12 he or she will have witnessed 8,000 murders and 100,000 acts of violence on television. *(Constitutional Rights Foundation, 7 July 2011)*

The American Academy of Child and Adolescent Psychiatry states that children, due to their violent viewing habits, are becoming *'immune to the horror of violence, gradually accept violence as a way to solve problems, imitate the violence they observe on television and identify with certain characters, victims and/or victimizers'*. Fear among children also increases as the amount of television viewing has increased. *(Media and Communication Studies Vol. 2(6), pp. 138-143, July 2010)*

The Bailey Review, commissioned by the Government, has warned that sexualised imagery is now *'a mainstream part of children's lives, forming the wallpaper or backdrop to their everyday activities'*. Mr Bailey stated that television programmes such as X-Factor, where the 2010 live final received thousands of public complaints about the sexually explicit dance routines by two female guest stars, need to improve their standards. The Review demanded that parents should have confidence that pre-watershed viewing (9pm) would be suitable for families. *(Letting Children be Children, 2011)*

The so-called watershed has been challenged for many years. Recent pre-watershed viewing has included murder, explicit hetero- and homo-sexual scenes, under-age sex, drug use, intimidation, explicit dancing, swearing and violence. Both BBC (2008) and ITV (2011) were reprimanded by Ofcom for broadcasting violent fight scenes in their pre-watershed flagship soaps EastEnders and Emmerdale. Both these soaps have a huge young fan base.

The BBC reported the case of two young brothers aged 10 and 12 years who pleaded guilty to a brutal attack on two younger boys aged 9 and 11 years. During the attack the older boy had a sink dropped on his head, one had a noose put around his head and one was burned with a cigarette on his eyelids and ear. The younger boy had a sharp stick rammed into his arm and cigarettes pushed into the wound. He also tried to ram a stick down his own throat after he was told to *'go away and kill himself'* by one of his attackers. They had bricks thrown at them and were repeatedly stamped on. Both boys were seriously injured. The brothers also admitted two counts of intentionally causing a child to engage in sexual activity. A relative of the guilty brothers alleged that their mother spiked their food with cannabis to make them sleep. The brothers grew up in a chaotic home watching horror movies from a young age. The relative said, *"From the age of about six or seven they used to watch horror movies, Chucky films, the sort that grown-ups daren't watch"*. *(BBC News, 3 September 2009)*

In 1993 when James Bulger was killed by two other children the nation reacted with shock and horror at what was, then, an unthinkable offence: children killing children. Knife crime, school shootings and violent assaults are becoming more commonplace amongst today's youth that are offending against other children.

Video gaming is a multibillion-pound industry and has many devoted and addicted followers. As technology has progressed video games have become incredibly sophisticated and disturbingly realistic. Some games require an online connection allowing children and teenagers to play with unknown adults who have an interest in role play, fantasy and violence.

Many of the most popular video games highlight harmful themes, promote the killing of people or animals, the use of drugs and alcohol, criminal behaviour, disregard for authority and the law, sexual exploitation and violence towards women, racial and sexual stereotyping, bad language, obscenities and obscene gestures. Some games have even included scenes of necrophilia, murder and engaging in the sex industry.

Children can become addicted and obsessed with video games which can create problems leading to poor social skills, isolation from family, lower educational achievements, exercising less, becoming overweight and aggressive thoughts and behaviours. *(American Academy of Child and Adolescent Psychiatry, 16 June 2011)*

Since 2001 England has dropped from third place to 19th in an international literacy league. Over the same period there has been a sharp rise in the amount of time children are spending in front of a screen, with one third of 10 year olds spending three hours or more each day playing on computers. *(Progress in International Reading Literacy Study, 2007)*

The fitness levels of British children are falling twice as fast as the global average. Less than one third of all children now play a competitive sport. This is partly due to the fact that they are using their spare time to play computer games, watch TV or use the internet. *(Archives of Disease in Childhood Journal, 2009)*

Whilst children watch television, engage in gaming or go online they are targeted by aggressive advertisers. Many advertisements are inappropriate for their age or are aimed at encouraging 'pester power' among children. A quarter of sites that children frequently use include advertisements that are aimed at adults including adult subjects such as online dating. Some advertisements have even included pictures of topless women. *(Fair Game, National Consumer Council, 2007)*

In research commissioned for the Children's Society *(2008)* 89% of adults felt that children are now more materialistic than in past generations, with children themselves saying that they feel under pressure to keep up with the latest trends. 90% of adults said that Christmas advertising aimed at children puts pressure on parents to spend more than they can afford.

Professor Philip Graham, Professor of Child Psychiatry at The Institute of Child Health, London, believes that commercial pressures may have worrying psychological effects on children: *"One factor that may be leading to rising mental health problems is the increasing degree to which children and young people are preoccupied with possessions; the latest in fashionable clothes and electronic equipment...Evidence both from the United States and from the UK suggests that those most influenced by commercial pressures also show higher rates of mental health problems".*

As adults we have to take responsibility for the current level of marketing aimed at our children. To blame children for being materialistic in a culture we have created is unjust. We are risking producing a generation who are left frustrated and unfulfilled through chasing an unattainable lifestyle. *(The Good Childhood Enquiry, 2008)*

Dr. Rowan Williams, the Archbishop of Canterbury, says: *"Children should be encouraged to value themselves for who they are as people rather than what they own. The selling of lifestyles to children creates a culture of material competitiveness and promotes acquisitive individualism at the expense of the principles of community and cooperation".* (The Children's Society, 2008)

8   Poisoned minds by what they read

- 42% of girls had been on strict diets. When asked why, 75% said that their strict dieting was to be attractive to others, with 66% claiming it was because of the media portrayal of women. *(Girls Attitude Survey, Girl Guiding UK, 2010)*

- 55% of parents think childhood is over by the time children start secondary school at 11. *(Random House Children's Books, 2008)*

- A 14 year old Salford boy pleaded guilty to raping four primary school girls in a park. The court was told how he was inspired to carry out the attacks by the violent sexual images he had seen. *(The Times, 24 March 2006)*

There has been an explosion in the teen and children's fiction market, with more authors targeting the 'youth pound'. Sadly, this has not raised standards. 'Doing It: do you remember your first time?' is a book written by Melvin Burgess aimed at young people. *'Dino really fancies fit, sexy Jackie but she just won't give him what he wants. Jonathan likes Deborah, but she's a bit fat – what will his mates say. Ben has been secretly shagging his teacher for ages. He used to love it, but what if he wants to stop?'* The front cover is of a female pair of legs with knickers pulled down. *(Doing It - ISBN: 9780141018034 Published 20 September 2004 by Penguin UK)*

Melvin Burgess helps to promote another book called 'Sugar Rush' by Julie Burchill. He says about the book *"A fabulous story of sexual fascination – guilt free, intoxicating and delicious. Sugar herself is a marvellous creation – promiscuous, immoral, manipulative, terrifying and oddly likeable. I only wish I had known her when I was her age and had the chance to be tossed aside like a used condom. But who am I kidding? She'd have scared me half to death"*. The book explores the world of teenage drugs and lesbians and has now been made into a Channel 4 series for children. *(Sugar Rush – ISBN-13: 978-0330415835 Published 6 May 2005, 2nd edition by Young Picador)*

A study by *The Sunday Telegraph* of several magazines aimed at teenage girls found that they contained sexually-explicit material which could infringe the magazine industry's editorial code. For example *Bliss* magazine (readers are on average aged 15 years) featured on one front cover the following stories: *The Sex Factor, your questions answered* and *Gang raped – for a mobile phone. Sugar* magazine, (readers aged 14 years on average) had a spread entitled *Is it a crush or are you gay?*

Top of the Pops Magazine, with readers aged 11-15 years, once promoted the magazine with a set of 'Kiss Me!' stickers. It also featured photos of topless male celebrities and a picture of an underwear model who appears to be naked except for a 'modesty' panel blanking out his genitals. *Bliss's* website has previously suggested girls send in photographs of themselves to be graded on '*looks and pullability*' in a contest coarsely named *How Sexy Am I? (The Daily Telegraph 14 March 2009)*

There is also a growing industry of 'lads' mags'. Though written for an adult audience, these are read by young boys. Publications such as *Nuts, FHM, Loaded* and *Zoo* magazines have feature titles such as '*Win a boob job for your girlfriend*' and offer '*Too Rude For TV*' DVDs featuring sex scenes that could not be shown on TV. *Zoo*, in the past, has promised '*girl on girl action*' and joked about women enjoying being urinated on and having sex with animals. Some encourage readers' girlfriends to send in explicit photos and seem to revel in the crude. *The Daily Sport* newspaper has regular pornographic images and stories available for just a few pence.

These publications are being sold in newsagents and supermarkets the length and breadth of our country within easy reach of children's comics. Many make significant amounts of money from advertisements for sex chat lines, sex shops and other adult services. The fear is that children as young as eight are gaining access to these magazines. On average 'lads' mags' have 70 topless photos per issue. *(BBC News, 27 June 2006)*

Premature sexualisation and pressure to grow up too quickly affects young girls' emotional well-being and mental health. Boys making sexual advances, pressure to wear provocative clothes and magazines that directly target young girls to lose weight or consider plastic surgery are taking their toll. Looking at pictures of models, pop stars and actresses made a fifth of girls interviewed feel sad, two-fifths feel bad about themselves and over a tenth feel angry by what they see. *(A Generation Under Stress, Girl Guiding UK, 2008)*

A class of 10 year olds at a Church of England primary school were asked by a teacher to write down the rudest words they could think of. Parents found a list of offensive and insulting words in their children's school books. Words ranged from variations on the F-word, crude slang for sex acts, female and male genitalia and racist and derogatory name-calling. The primary school children were encouraged to come up with a list of hurtful words that victims of bullying might be subjected to. A parent complained *"Some of the words used were so bad, I'd never heard them before and the whole episode beggars belief"*. *(The Daily Telegraph, 18 February 2009)*

The General Teaching Council (*November 2008*) expressed their support for the 'No Outsiders' project based in primary schools and funded by The Economic and Social Research Council. Teachers developed strategies and resources to address lesbian, gay, bisexual and transgender equality in their own *primary* education settings. The material includes puppets, plays and fairy-tales aimed at teaching children as young as four about same-sex relationships. It is well established by psychologists that children between the ages of 6 and 12 years are in a 'latency' period and that premature introduction of sexual material during this period can disrupt natural sexual development.

Popular comedian David Walliams was short listed for a prestigious literary prize after writing a book on a cross-dressing school boy. Walliams says of his book *"In a small way it is about sexual awakening"*. The book is aimed at 7 year old children. *(Daily Telegraph, 8 September 2009)*

Most parents are oblivious to the content of the magazines, books and internet sites that their children are reading. Sadly, most children no longer have innocent memories of childhood. Stories of adventure, intrigue and moral guidance have now been shattered with horror, sex and violence.

9 Poisoned minds by what they hear

- Two thirds of all sexual references in music are degrading in nature. 45% of teenagers who listen to large amounts of sexually explicit songs are sexually active. *(Primack, BA et al, American Journal of Preventive Medicine, 2009, 36: (4) 317-323)*

- 39% of school teachers claim to have been abused with sexual swearing and 75% of pupils are aiming sexually abusive swearing at each other. *(A Serious Business: NUT & University of Warwick Survey, 2006)*

- Record numbers of people are complaining about the use of foul language on TV and radio programmes. Complaints have increased almost 40%. *(The Christian Institute, 5 May 2010)*

Teenagers are greatly influenced by music. The music industry continues to use this to their advantage. Music often dictates language, lifestyle, behaviour and even morality. Jimi Hendrix (who died of a drugs overdose aged 27) said in 'Life Magazine' *"You can hypnotise with music and when you get people at the weakest point you can preach into the subconscious what you want to say".* (2 October 1969)

Teenagers who listen to music with sexual lyrics start having sex sooner than those who prefer other songs. Songs that portray men as sexually promiscuous, women as sex objects and with explicit references to sex acts are more likely to prompt early sexual behaviour than those where sexual references are more muted and where relationships appear more committed. *(Brown JD et al, Pediatrics, vol 117, No 4, April 2006, 1018-1027)*

Teenagers who said they listened to lots of music with degrading sexual messages were almost twice as likely to start having sex or experiment with other sexual activities within the following two years than teenagers who listened to little or no sexually degrading music. *(Martino SC et al, Pediatrics, Vol 118, No 2, August 2006, e430-e441)*

One 17 year old girl spoke of listening to sexually explicit music saying that she and other teens sometimes listen to sexually explicit songs because they like the beat. She went on to say *"I won't really realize that the person is talking about having sex or raping a girl"* but she feels like the message *"is being beaten into the teens' heads. We don't even really realize how much"*. *(msnbc.com, 7 August 2006)*

The music industry has become so sexualised and morally corrupted that a review commissioned by the government has suggested that an age rating should be considered. This is to ensure that inappropriate music is not sold to children and that parents can make more informed choices about what they allow their children to buy. *(The Bailey Review, June 2011)*.

It becomes clear why the above recommendation was made on listening to some of the lyrics from mainstream songs. Popular songs played daily on our radios include lyrics such as: *'Come here rude boy, boy; can you get it up? Come here rude boy, boy; is you big enough? Take it, take it baby, baby take it, take it; Love me, love me Tonight, I'ma give it to ya harder...'*. *(Rihanna, Rude Boy, Def Jam)*

A different song called S&M by the same artists has the lyrics *'Feels so good being bad, There's no way I'm turning back, Now the pain is my pleasure, Cause nothing could measure......The affliction of the feeling, Leaves me wanting more, Cause I may be bad, But I'm perfectly good at it, Sex in the air, I don't care, I love the smell of it, Sticks and stones, may break my bones, But chains and whips, excite me'*. *(Rihanna, S&M, Def Jam)*

*'I got a dirty mind I got filthy ways....I be so far up, We don't give a f***.......You're so hypnotizing, could you be the devil....Kiss me, kiss me, Infect me with your love and, Fill me with your poison, Take me, take me, Wanna be a victim...Tell me what's next, alien sex. I'ma disrobe you, Than, I'mma probe you, See I abducted you, So I tell ya what to do'*. *(Katy Perry & Kanye West, ET, Capitol)* These lyrics are just a small selection and are by no means unique.

Heavy metal music often glorifies drug use, murder, suicide and Satanism. It debases human relations, degrades sex and is fundamentally aggressive. The literature associated with the music is littered with blasphemy and obscene language. This typically graphic song by *Possessed* is an example of the lyrics fans of the genre listen to. *'Arise from the dead and attack from the grave, The killing won't stop until first light. We'll bring you to hell because we want to enslave...Lay down the laws from our satanic scripts...Lucifer laughs, his needs are fulfilled...Bodies are burning, the people are killed, Torture the reason we fought....Blood's what we want and we won't settle, Until we drive you insane, Attacking the young and killing the old, Bleeding with every heart beat....Know that your life is at its end, Rendered helpless so scream out fright'.* (Possessed, Death Metal, Relativity)

On 23 September 2008 a school shooting took place in Finland when a student in the local polytechnic entered his school, shot 10 people and finally himself. The perpetrator, 18 year old Matti Saari, had posted videos of himself on the internet threatening to kill people *(Ministry of Justice, Finland, 2010)*. Saari was a passionate follower of 'goth' music that used the holocaust, child murder and Nazis as inspiration. He listened to musicians whose song titles include 'Slave to Evil', 'Death Maker' and 'Line of Corpses'. His main interests were horror films and guns. Saari had developed an unhealthy interest in other school shootings, downloading what he could on them from the internet. *(Daily Telegraph, 24 September 2008)*

A subgenre of hip hop music is gangsta rap. It glorifies rape, urban crime, incites racial hatred and gang violence. Young people with a high exposure to rap music were three times more likely to hit a teacher and more than two and a half times as likely to have been arrested when compared with their peers who listened to less rap music. They were also twice as likely to have multiple sexual partners and more than one and a half times as likely to get a STI, use drugs and use alcohol. *(Wingood GM et al. American Journal of Public Health, 2003, 93: 437-439)*

Leading music stars are held up as the idols of the day. They are emulated, adored and idolised. Yet they are often not a benchmark that any parent would want their children to use as a guide for life. They often have extremely chaotic lives, broken relationships, a casual approach to commitments such as marriage, openly use drugs and are relentless in their pursuit of fame and adoration. Often those who die young become cult-like figures to the young who want to imitate their idols.

In a poll commissioned for BBC's Panorama 55% of people questioned said swearing on TV is at an *'unacceptable'* level, 68% said that swearing on programmes had increased in the last five years, 58% said that broadcasters do not take enough notice of audience views on the amount of swearing on TV and radio and 41% said that they did not think the watershed was being effectively enforced. The poll was commissioned following a media scandal over offensive calls made by popular presenters Jonathan Ross and Russell Brand on Brand's BBC Radio 2 show. The pair left vulgar voicemail messages for 78 year old Andrew Sachs about his granddaughter. This pre-recorded programme was then aired. *(BBC Panorama, Jan 2009)*

This poisoning of the minds of children and young people has now become an established element of contemporary society. It needs to be recognised that the influences on children and young people have become more consistently negative and destructive than ever before.

10 Exploited by drug traffickers

- 19.3% of 16-24 year olds in the UK used illicit drugs in the last year. 37.7% (2.5 million) have used illicit drugs during their life time. *(Home Office 2011/12)*

- 21,955 under 18's accessed specialist substance misuse services in the UK in 2010-11. 128 were under the age of 12 years and 315 were aged 12-13 years. *(National Drug Treatment Monitoring System 2012)*

- There is a strong link between STIs, sexual behaviour and drug use. The links between substance use and risky sexual behaviour are considerable. *(Independent Advisory Group on Sexual Health and HIV, 2007)*

- In one year in Scotland a total of 254 children lost a parent or parental figure from a drug-related death. 59 children were living with a person who died from a drug-related death. *(The National Drug Related Death Database Scotland, 2009)*

Findings from an NHS survey indicate that in England in 2009 around 250,000 children had taken drugs (including glue, gas and other volatile substances) in the previous month and around 450,000 had taken drugs in the last year. Thirty three percent of children have been offered drugs at some point in their lives. *(The Information Centre for Health and Social Care, July 2010)*.

2.5% of the UK population are users of cocaine. This is one of the highest usage rates of the drug in Europe. The highest rate is in those aged 15-34 with up to 8% of this age group using cocaine. In terms of the health consequences of drug use, almost 18% of those who inject drugs are HIV positive. This means that worldwide nearly one in five injecting drug users are living with HIV. *(United Nations Office on Drugs and Crime World Drug Report, 2011)*

Statistics on drugs use show that, surprisingly, almost a quarter of the UK's school-age children (11-15 years) have tried drugs. This figure is much higher than in Europe.   13% of UK under-13s have tried cannabis. The European average is 4%. The trend for drugs use in school children remained stable across Europe between 1999 and 2005. In the UK it doubled. *(BRAHA, Drugs Culture, June 2009. Source: Institute of Alcohol Studies, Alcohol Alert No.1, 2009)*

Many are arguing for the legalising of cannabis claiming that its use is no more dangerous than that of cigarette smoking. Yet the immediate effects of use include confusion, hallucinations, anxiety and paranoia. Cannabis use may also interfere with a person's ability to concentrate, organise and use information, with this effect seeming to last several weeks after use. This makes work or study difficult and cannabis use in adolescence is linked to poor performance at school.

A recently published study of cannabis users over a 25 year period has found that those who started using cannabis before the age of 18 years suffered a drop in IQ.   The level of IQ reduction was directly related to the amount of cannabis smoked.   They also found that stopping or reducing cannabis use failed to fully restore the lost IQ. *(Proceedings of the National Academy of Sciences 2012)*

There is mounting evidence that people with serious mental illness, including depression and psychosis, are more likely to use cannabis or have used it for long periods of time previously. Regular users of the drug are two times more likely to have a psychotic episode or develop schizophrenia. Research has suggested that there is a clear link between early cannabis use and later mental health problems. Children who use cannabis daily were five times more likely to develop depression and anxiety in later life. Starting to smoke cannabis before the age of 15 is associated with a four-fold increase in the likelihood of developing a psychotic disorder by the age of 26 years. *(The Royal College of Psychiatrists, 16 June 2011. Source: Fontes MA et al, British Journal of Psychiatry 2011, 198: 442-447)*

Drug abuse is growing. There were 1,037 PNDs (penalty notice for disorder) issued for drug offences in 2008/09 compared with 14,570 in 2010/11 and 80,658 Cannabis Warnings were issued.   Overall there were 232,216 drug offences in the same period. *(Crimes Detected in England and Wales, Home Office, 2011)*

The immediate cost of crime committed by young people misusing drugs and alcohol is just under £100m per year. *(Department for*

Education, February 2011). Yet the deeper cost is being felt as our children suffer the consequences of drug abuse. Increased risk of HIV, mental health problems, increased sexual promiscuity, vulnerability to exploitation and abuse and even death are the penalties they face. There were 250 ecstasy-related deaths reported between 1999 and 2004. The victims were mostly young. *(Office for National Statistics, Spring 2005)*

An 18 year old boy was jailed for life after killing two other teenagers. The teenager, Thomas Palmer, claimed to be mentally ill at the time of the killings. An expert witness for the prosecution said that his psychotic symptoms were likely to have been caused by his heavy cannabis use. He had been smoking skunk in the weeks before the killings and had become increasingly paranoid. *(Daily Telegraph, 27 July 2007)*

The illegal drugs trade in the UK generates about £8bn annually *(The Independent, 14 July 2012).* Of organised crime groups 56% are involved in drug trafficking. Organised crime leads to misery for the numerous people affected by it. It involves human trafficking, prostitution and drugs. Its knock-on effects are burglary, car crime and muggings which are often carried out to fund drug habits. *(BBC News, Life of Crime, 16 July 2011)*

It is estimated that more than 350,000 children live with a parent who has a drug problem. *(Addaction, 2012)*

Children are living with drug-addicted parents and with parents or family members who deal drugs. Children are literally caught up in the cross-fire associated with drug culture. Joel Smith shot dead Toni-Anne Byfield, aged 7 years, in the back as she ran away from him. She had just witnessed the murder of her drug dealer father by Smith. *(The Times, 4 August 2006)*

Children pay a high price in our society, which now accepts drug use as inevitable. Accidental poisonings are increasing with children's lives being put at risk through the accidental ingestion of drugs kept in their homes.

Children are being forced into working as drug mules. *(UNICEF, 16 July 2011)* A 12 year old boy flew thousands of miles to the USA carrying heroin worth £700,000 in his stomach. He needed surgery to remove the drugs from his colon and save his life. *(Daily Mail, 15 July 2011)*

An 11-year old, Carl Benjamin, lives on one of the most deprived estates in the UK and dreams of being a doctor when he is older. He is worried that all the trouble on his estate and in his school might stop him from achieving his dream. *"You get used to living with a lot of crime. I've had to run away from drunkards and people high on drugs lots of times because they've been chasing me. We always have drug dealers hanging around in our back garden too. They're always messing up the garden and smashing our windows".* (Crimestoppers UK, 16 July 2011)

Our society has accepted and promoted role models for our children who are unhelpful in the face of attempts to control drug abuse. Noel Gallagher, a member of the pop group Oasis said, in defence of a fellow pop star's use of drugs, *"As soon as people realise that the majority of people in this country take drugs, then the better off we'll all be. It's not like a scandalous sensation or anything like that…drugs is like getting up and having a cup of tea in the morning".* *(BBC Radio, January 1997).* This man remains famous, influential and in the public eye to this day. Children are exposed to this kind of message every time they open a magazine, log on to the internet or follow a 'tweet'.

11 Abused and Corrupted

- There were 50,552 children on child-protection registers or the subject of child-protection plans in the UK by the end of March 2011. This has increased from 32,492 in 2006. *(NSPCC Inform, 2012)*

- In 2009-10 the number of sexual crimes against children under 16 years recorded in England and Wales was 16,864. *(Home Office, 2010)*

- There were 2,500 subjects of a child protection plan during 2009-10 due to sexual abuse in England alone. *(Department for Education, 2010)*

- Almost 20% of sexual abuse against children is carried out by a woman. *(Childline Case notes on sexual abuse, November 2009)*

- One in three female prison inmates claims to have been the victim of sexual abuse. *(Women in Prison, 21 July 2011)*

Of all sexual crimes recorded in England and Wales in 2009-10 31% were against children under 16 years. This totalled 16,864. More than one third of all rapes recorded by police in this period were committed against children. *(Home Office, Crime in England and Wales 2009-2010: findings from the British Crime Survey and police recorded crime Table 2. May, 2010)*

The impact and devastation that sexual abuse has on children is still not realised by the Criminal Justice System. Keith Fenn (2007) was given only a 32 months sentence after twice raping a 10 year old girl in a park. In 2011 another judge told a court that two 12 year olds 'wanted sex' with six young footballers and so released the men after they had been found guilty of gang-raping the girls. These derisory sentences are not only failing to protect our children but also reflect the fact that sexual abuse is not being viewed as seriously as it should be.

Children are crying out to be heard. Childline has taken literally thousands of calls from desperate children. The following are examples of recorded calls:

"Last night when I was in the toilet, my mum's boyfriend came in and sexually abused me. I don't want to tell mum, because she won't believe me". Girl, aged eight.

"My mum has a drinking problem. When she drinks too much she comes into my room, undresses me and makes me have sex with her". Boy, aged 14.

"Dad has been sexually abusing me and my sister. My mum died when I was four years old. I feel bad when he abuses me". Girl, aged nine.

"I am physically and sexually abused at home by mum. It has been happening since I was two years old. I feel sad". Girl, aged 12

"I am being sexually abused by my brother. My mum and dad don't believe me. My parents think it is my fault and I must have led him on or come on to him. I am told to keep this a secret and I am struggling to cope with this". Girl, aged 12. *(Childline Case notes on sexual abuse, November 2009)*

The Deputy Children's Commissioner, Sue Berelowitz, has been given the task of investigating the sexualisation of our children. Giving evidence to the House of Commons Home Affairs Committee she said *"There are parts of London where certainly children expect to have to perform oral sex on line-ups of boys, up to two hours at a time from the age of 11.......it is quite common for girls to be lured via internet chat rooms to meet a friend, only to be met by a group of boys and gang-raped in a park. Then another group of boys come, they take her to another part of the park and she is serially raped again.... I wish I could say to you that such things are uncommon but I'm afraid they are quite common"*. *(12 June 2012)*

Often it is assumed that children who have suffered abuse can recover from their trauma. To think this is naive in the extreme. Children who have been sexually abused suffer a range of long-term physical, emotional and psychological problems that persist even when the abuse has stopped. The effects almost always continue through to adulthood and often throughout the person's life.

Effects can include: loss of confidence, dignity and self respect, low self-esteem and poor self-worth, loss of hope for the future, adverse effects on both physical and mental health, the inability to trust others (even close family and friends), the inability to relax and enjoy life, loss of innocence and childhood, anxiety, guilt and fear and difficulties in relating to the opposite sex. Sexual abuse may also lead to alcohol and drug abuse, obsessive behaviour and strict routines, anxiety states, self-harming, depression and suicide. *(Breathing Space Scotland, 21 July 2011)*

The abuse of children is widespread in British society. The NSPCC has found that one in four 18-24 year olds had been physically attacked by an adult during childhood, sexually assaulted, or severely neglected at home. One in seven had been severely maltreated by a parent or guardian. One in nine young adults had suffered severe physical abuse as a child at the hands of an adult, which included being hit, kicked, beaten or attacked with a weapon.

One in nine young adults reported they had been sexually assaulted as a child, either by an adult or another child or young person and 3% had suffered sexual abuse involving physical contact at the hands of a boyfriend or a girlfriend. Almost one in 10 young adults had been severely neglected by parents or guardians during childhood. *(NSPCC, Child Cruelty in the UK, 2011)* Other studies suggest that as many as one in four girls and one in six boys are sexually assaulted at some point before they reach the age of 18.

One NSPCC research participant, Pete, said *"Over the years, my mum kicked and beat me, she throttled me, threw me down the stairs, pushed me into a scalding hot bath. She once held my head under water and another time she shoved a full bar of soap in my mouth. There are too many incidents to recount. For a long time, I accepted what was going on at home as normal. But no child should have to live in fear or on edge in their own home – that's the place they should feel safest".*

The US government *(2008)* suggests that as many as 80% of young adults who had been abused or neglected as children met the diagnostic criteria for at least one psychiatric disorder by the age of 21. These young adults exhibited many problems, including depression, anxiety, eating disorders and suicide attempts. Other psychological and emotional conditions associated with abuse and neglect include panic disorders, dissociative disorders, attention-deficit disorder, depression, anger and post-traumatic stress disorder.

Abused and neglected children are 11 times more likely to be youth offenders, 2.7 times more likely to be arrested for violent and criminal behaviour as an adult and 3.1 times more likely to be arrested for one of many forms of violent crime. The cycle continues through the generations. Abusive parents have often experienced abuse during their own childhoods. It is estimated approximately one-third of abused and neglected children will eventually victimize their own children. *(Long Term Consequences of Child Abuse and Neglect, US Government, 2008)*

'Sexting' is defined as the *'exchange of sexual messages or images and creating, sharing and forwarding sexually suggestive nude or nearly nude images through mobile phones and the internet'*. The NSPCC found that up to 40% of children have been involved in this. Coercion from their peers was found to be a factor in 'sexting'. These threats are often linked to harassment, bullying and even violence. *(NSPCC, A qualitative study of children, young people and 'sexting', 2012)* These images are in essence child pornography.

A 16 year old boy pleaded guilty to making indecent images of a child after using his mobile phone to film his friend having sex with a 14 year old girl. He sent it to five of her classmates. A further two 16 year old schoolboys were arrested for making a porn video on a mobile phone of a 14 year old girl and circulating it around their school in Perth.

There are pressure groups that want to legalise sexual relationships between adults and children. One group, the North American Man/Boy Lover Association (NAMBLA), has stated that its mission is to remove the age of consent and wants those jailed for sexual offences against children to be released. It is well recognised that trends established in the USA quickly follow in the UK.

Systematic and planned abuse of children is also frequently part of extreme occult practice. Despite the protests that ritual abuse doesn't happen it is something that can no longer be denied. Children are being subjected to the most appalling assaults imaginable.

In March 2001, in a Welsh Court, Colin Batley was found guilty of 35 sex offences against children and young adults. The assaults were part of Satanist ritual abuse in a coven he led. His wife, Elaine, was also found guilty of sexual activity and indecency towards children. Victims were also 'initiated' (repeatedly sexually abused) during 'black masses' at the Batleys' home. He dressed up in hooded robes, chanting before an altar where he took part in sexual activity with women and children as young as 11 years. At least two of his victims gave birth as a result of the abuse they suffered. Some of the Batleys' neighbours involved in the coven paid him 25% of their income as a sign of devotion. The children were threatened with death and intimidated into keeping quiet.

In 2001 the torso of an African boy aged between four and seven, was found in the River Thames. The boy, named Adam by police, is thought to have been the victim of a ritualistic killing after being brought to London from Nigeria. In the ongoing investigation police found that 300 black African boys had disappeared from London between July and September 2001 suggesting that the trafficking of children, for a variety of reasons, was a serious problem. A decade on, Adam has not been forgotten as authorities continue to investigate.

Six people were arrested and accused of sedating and sexually abusing 15 children, some as young as three. The group included three women teachers. Two of the women are grandmothers. The group are accused of filming them in sexual acts with satanic overtones at the teachers' homes and in a wood. The alleged abuse was discovered when some of the children began talking about their 'games' to their parents. They drew pictures of a *man in black* who wore a hood and drank his own blood. They were threatened that if they told their parents about the 'games', they would be *'taken away from their mothers by devils'*. (The Times, 26 April 2007)

Erratum
The first line on page 43 should read:

In March 2011, in a Welsh Court...

12 Exploited by Pornographers

- Recorded offences of abuse of children through prostitution and pornography in England and Wales in 2009/10 numbered 135. *(Home Office, 2010)*

- About one million indecent images of children were discovered at a house in East London. It is the largest seizure the Metropolitan Police's Paedophile Unit has ever made from one individual. *(Sky News, 16 July 2011)*

- The Internet Watch Foundation took action regarding 16,739 instances of child sexual abuse content during 2010 on different web pages around the world. *(Internet Watch Foundation. Annual Report, 2010)*

Child pornography is not a victimless crime as each indecent image of a child possessed or distributed represents a child that has been abused in order that the image can be made. With the advent of internet child pornography it has become easier to distribute and share images. This multiplies the sickening horror of child abuse and torture by circulating the degradation of children to feed deviant behaviour and make vast sums of money.

UNICEF continues to campaign for children across the world who are being exploited by child pornographers. Their study found that digital technology not only allows traffickers to recruit children, but makes it easier to distribute pornography through e-mail, chat rooms and e-groups. *'It is happening that children are being used as sex toys – those children are being used as sex commodities. The younger they are, the more saleable they are'. (Combating child sexual exploitation in the Philippines pornography trade, 2008)*

A huge increase in child pornography has taken place due to the internet. Many paedophiles have acknowledged that introduction to child pornography encourages their sexual fantasies and is an important factor in leading them to commit actual sexual offences against children. Organised crime also uses child pornography, to generate vast amounts of revenue. *(Child Abuse and the Internet: 'Safeguarding Children and Young People' North East Regional Interagency Procedures Project, 2005)*

The internet allows larger numbers of individuals to network and get involved in collecting and possessing images of child abuse. It is, therefore, highly likely that an increasing number of children are being abused specifically for this purpose. Every time an image is viewed and re-viewed the child in that image is violated all over again. *(Child abuse, child pornography and the internet, National Children's Homes, January 2004)*

The link between child pornography and the actual physical abuse of children cannot be ignored. Daniel Taylor, 31 years old, was found with 300,000 images of child pornography. Police found his instruction video for paedophiles on how to abuse children and *'not leave a trace'* and a covert camera disguised as a cigarette lighter capable of capturing and storing video. He also admitted 20 counts of making indecent images, four of taking indecent images and two counts of sexual assault on a baby. *(AOL News, 4 August 2011)*

Child pornography is available on home computers, mobile phones and a dizzying array of other multi-media devices. Often this is unsolicited material. Children as young as six are surfing the internet without parental supervision. 14% of 6-10 year olds have encountered adult-based material on the net. *(TalkTalk, 2011)*

Children today live in a society where hard-core pornography is easy to procure. Our children are being seduced daily through a medium we allow into our homes and often our children's bedrooms. Pornography negatively affects girls as well as boys and can considerably damage their ability to form healthy relationships. *(Focus on the Family, 7 August 2011)*

Children are vulnerable to predators who use pornography to 'groom' their victims. As in cases of child abuse, the Criminal Justice System further devalues abused children by the derisory sentences it gives for the crime of child pornography.

A married father was found with more than one million child pornography images on his computer. He was given a one year suspended sentence, escaping prison. This is despite some of the collection including images of children under the age of 10. *(Leeds Crown Court, March 2012)*

With the arrival of the digital age child pornography can haunt a child victim for the rest of their lives. The abuse and torture they suffered is digitally immortalised prolonging the agony of their abuse.

13 Exploited by Prostitution

- At any one time across the world, around 1.8 million children are being abused through prostitution, child pornography and sex tourism. In the UK there are an estimated 5,000 child prostitutes. *(Save the Children, March 2007)*

- Mexico's social service reports that there are more than 16,000 children engaged in prostitution. The tourist destinations have the highest number. *(UNICEF, Child Trafficking, 2009)*

- An average serial child molester may have as many as 400 victims in his or her lifetime. *(Child Sexual Abuse Prevention Study; notificationisprevention.org; 2009)*

- A conservative estimate suggests that child prostitutes serve between two and thirty clients per week, leading to an appalling estimate of anywhere between 100 and 1,500 clients per year, per child. Younger children, many below the age of 10, are increasingly drawn into prostitution. *(US Department of Justice, Child Sex Trade, 8 August 2011)*

Child prostitution is an established worldwide problem and continues to grow in the UK. The FBI agent John Gillies states, *"The money involved in prostituting children is much higher than just regular prostitution"*. *(CBN, November 2009)*

"Today, more than twice as many people are in bondage around the world than were taken in chains during the entire 350 years of the African slave trade. Despite the abolition of slavery, modern forms of trading in human beings continue, whether for sexual exploitation, forced labour, domestic slavery or organised crime... In the United Kingdom, many thousands of individuals are bought and sold as commodities and forced into modern-day slavery. This is commonly known as human trafficking". *(Anthony Steen MP, House of Commons, 5 February 2010)*

One British case of nine men on trial described girls as young as 13 used for prostitution. 55 charges, included inciting child prostitution, grooming and rape by six married men and one grandfather. Seven of the girls, from troubled backgrounds, were more vulnerable. Girls were passed around as sexual commodities. They received cash, alcohol, drugs, meals and mobile phone credit as their payment. One girl was 14 weeks pregnant but continued to be sold for sex. It is not known what happened to the baby. *(Daily Mail, 15 June 2011)* This story is not unique in Britain today.

Although child sex tourism has existed for many years, the practice has exploded due to the internet and the growth of the tourist industry. Special packages exist for Western tourists where the sole purpose of the holiday is to have sex with children. Sex tour organisers also use the internet to distribute child pornography and advertise sex tours.

'Maria is prostituted by her aunt. Maria is obliged to sell her body exclusively to foreign tourists in Costa Rica, she only works mornings as she has to attend school in the afternoon. Maria is in fifth grade'. (US Department of Justice, Child Sex Trade, 8 August 2011)

Child sex tourism is a lucrative multi-billion dollar industry that is fuelled by greed and corruption. It involves organised crime syndicates and international trafficking networks. Many poor nations rely on sex trafficking as a source of income and may have a vested interest in turning a blind eye to the suffering of their children. In countries such as Indonesia, Malaysia, the Philippines and Thailand the sex industry accounts for anywhere between 2% and 14% of national income. *(Children as Tourist Attractions, Song S, Youth International Resource Paper 9 August 2011)*

"I started as a sex worker because of one of our neighbours....Normally, the oldest men come to me. I think that they are mostly over 40 years old....I want to stop doing this, but I don't know how because my mother needs the money. I don't want to continue because then I know that I won't have an education, but I need to help feed my family". Shetra, age 13. *(UNICEF, 8 August 2011)*

Some paedophiles justify their abuse of children by claiming that they are helping the child and its family to escape economic hardship. *"On this trip, I've had sex with a 14 year old girl in Mexico and a 15 year old in Colombia. I'm helping them financially. If they don't have sex with me, they may not have enough food. If someone has a problem with me doing this, let UNICEF feed them".* Retired schoolteacher. *(US Department of Justice, Child Sex Trade, 8 August 2011)*

British nationals who are convicted for sexual offences abroad can travel back to the UK undetected and unknown. This presents a very significant risk to children in the UK. *(Off the Radar, Protecting Children from British Sex Offenders who Travel. ECPAT UK, February 2011)*

"Sexual exploitation leaves children with psychological and at times physical scars, and diminishes their hopes of leading a life of dignity...No country or region is immune, and there are no innocent bystanders". (UNICEF Executive Director Ann M. Veneman. *Rio de Janeiro, Brazil 2008)*

ECPAT have said traffickers instil terror in their victims in order to have psychological control of the child. The methods used to intimidate the children include physical and sexual violence and emotional abuse and neglect. Some children, especially girls brought to the UK for sexual exploitation, are likely to be brutally raped as part of an initiation rite. Frequently children are made to watch other children being beaten or assaulted. Often children are kept isolated and in unspeakable conditions. Many of these children are forced into debt bondage, paying back money that has been used to bring them to the UK, a place they were desperate to get to for a better life. Some children will be told that they can leave as soon as they have repaid their debt but their debt never lessens. Passports and other identity documents are taken from them. Both boys and girls are trafficked for sexual exploitation. *(The trafficking of children for sexual exploitation, ECPAT UK, 2009)*

Children used in this way are vulnerable, alone in a country where they may not know the language, have no knowledge of the system that is there to protect them and live in fear for their lives. They are isolated, broken, violated and abused. They are considered expendable, hidden from society and are left with no hope for the future.

The lives of child prostitutes are appalling. They live in constant fear of sadistic acts by clients, fear of being beaten by pimps who control the sex trade and fear of the authorities. Many victims of child sexual prostitution suffer from physical disorders. These include tuberculosis, exhaustion, infections, physical injuries resulting from cruelty inflicted upon them and sexually transmitted diseases. Living conditions are horrendous and food infrequent. Children who do not earn enough money are punished ruthlessly. Drug use and suicide are common amongst victims of child sexual exploitation. Victims often suffer from depression, low self-esteem and feelings of hopelessness. *(US Department of Justice, Child Sex Trade, 8 August 2011)*

Unwanted pregnancy, sexually transmitted diseases and HIV are all issues child prostitutes deal with daily. There is a strong myth in some cultures that HIV/AIDS can be cured through sex with a virgin leading to children becoming more vulnerable. *(UNICEF, Child Trafficking, 2009)* This appalling fabrication has led to very young children and babies being raped.

An HIV-positive former German musician went on trial charged with abusing seven children and 23 youths in Thailand. The 65 year old was accused of 403 cases of unprotected sex with child prostitutes, despite knowing he was HIV positive. Due to his HIV status, which he allegedly did not reveal, the man is also accused of attempting to infect his victims. *(Thai Visa.com, December 2010)*

Children are being treated as commodities, being violated, tortured and abused in order to meet the sick demands of an ever growing trade. This reprehensible trade brings shame on all humanity.

14 Morally Corrupted

- More than 1,000 girls aged 11-12 and 58,000 15 year olds have been prescribed the contraceptive pill by doctors. *(Sunday Times, 1 August 2010)*

- After government spending of £300 million on its Teenage Pregnancy Strategy, there was a spectacular failure to reduce teenage pregnancy and abortion rates. *(Too Much, Too Young, Christian Institute, 2010)*

- The earlier a woman begins sexual activity, the more sexual partners she is likely to have during her lifetime. *(Rector RE et al. The Heritage Foundation, June 2003)*

- Deprivation is a significant predictor in binge drinking. In the North West alone it is calculated that around 56,900 binge drink at least weekly. *(Centre for Public Health, March 2008)*

- Children who see their parents drunk are twice as likely to get drunk regularly themselves. *(Joseph Rowntree Trust, 2011)*

- Having sex at an early age can double the risk of developing cervical cancer. *(Louie KS et al. British Journal of Cancer, 2009, 100: 1191-1197)*

The key issues of morality are today being marginalised and there is a real confusion amongst children on basic moral behaviour. The breakdown of the family and lack of community support means that children and young people are deprived of any moral compass on which to model their lives.

An NHS publication tells school pupils they have a 'right' to an enjoyable sex life and that it is good for their health. The booklet *(Pleasure, 2009)* says experts focus too much on the need for safe sex and loving relationships but not enough on the pleasure it can bring. One heading reads *'an orgasm a day keeps the doctor away'*. The leaflet goes on to say: *'Health promotion experts advocate five portions of fruit and veg a day and 30 minutes physical activity three times a week. What about sex or masturbation twice a week?'* This advice seems to ignore the fact that the UK has one of the highest rates of underage pregnancies in Europe, abortion rates are soaring and STI levels are at an all time high.

Materials in schools are sexualizing our children under the guise of sex education. Materials such as this have been recommended by several local authorities:

For age 5 years plus: *'Mummy Laid an Egg'* (B. Cole). Several diagrams of sexual positions their parents may have used to conceive them. These diagrams are made 'child friendly' by making them appear to be drawn by a child. *'How Did I Begin?'* (M. Manning & B. Granström). Alongside drawings of adults having sex text describing what is happening.

For age 7 years plus: *'Where Did I Come From?'* (P Mayle). Beside drawings of adults having sex are drawings of children playing, description of what sex should feel like and comments like this: *'Making love is like skipping. You can do it all day long'.*

The Primary School Sex and Relationships Education Pack recommends word-meaning games using 'key terms' like anal intercourse, bisexual, incest, masturbation, oral sex and prostitution. These examples are by no means unusual. Other materials, recommended for primary school use, include cartoon videos of people having sex, graphic sexual imagery and descriptions. They discuss homosexuality and encourage experimentation. *(Too Much, Too Young, Christian Institute, 2010)*

Most secondary schools across Bolton have a nurse drop-in service that will also provide condoms as part of the 'condom promotion' scheme. Young people can access a range of free condoms on production of a scheme membership card. *(Sexual Health Bolton, 2011)* The clinics are mostly based in schools. The facility is anonymous and parents remain uninformed of the advice and access to services their child is given.

Children and young people are not being told the whole truth about the consequences of premature sexual activity. Condoms are being distributed to children with the message 'as long as it's safe sex is ok'.

Condoms may reduce the chance of pregnancy and STIs. However, they are certainly not 100% effective, especially when used by children. Condom use reduces the risk of HIV transmission by 85%, but for STIs like gonorrhoea and chlamydia the risk reduction is only around 50%. Even when using contraceptives 15% to 20% of teenagers become pregnant. *(Malhotra S. Impact of the Sexual Revolution, Journal of American Physicians and Surgeons, 2008 13: (3) 82-87)*

A girl needs permission from doctors to have her appendix removed but can be prescribed the pill or have an abortion without the knowledge of her parents. Children are at risk of being unsupported, abused and even physically at risk when left alone to deal with these adult issues.

Two 13 year old pupils were excluded from a top £30,000 a year private school for having a sexual encounter in a sandpit. A second boy has been thrown out for stealing whisky from a Waitrose store as part of the same incident. *(Daily Mail, 20 July 2011)*

11% of teachers reported that they had experienced sexual harassment from pupils at some point in their careers. One female teacher commented that she had to suffer one *"...particular pupil making sexual comments about me and my appearance"*. Another said that while walking past a group of 14 year old boys she heard one of them say, untruthfully, *"Is that the teacher you had in the cupboard?"* and reported *"wolf whistling and hissing at me then a few, maybe three shouted 'I'll do ya!'"*. *(NUT Policy Statement on preventing sexual harassment and bullying, 2007)*

We are lying to our children by telling them that sexual morality is a thing of the past and is an outdated concept that has no relevance today. The sexualisation of society encourages our young to experiment sexually and implies there are no consequences. Health studies show that the healthiest women are those whose sexual activity is solely within a married relationship. Women who have more non-marital sex partners are more likely to be single mothers, are at an increased risk of STIs, abortion and have lower levels of personal happiness than women who had only ever had sex with their husbands. *(The Heritage Foundation, June 2003)*

Alcohol is one of the main reasons for young people having sex. They report that they are more likely to have unprotected sex when they are under the influence of alcohol. Girls aged 16 years who binge drink and those drinking greater amounts (over 40 units) each week, were two and a half times more likely to have had sex they later regretted after drinking alcohol. Binge drinking youths were also more likely to have been involved in violence following use of alcohol. *(Centre for Public Health, March 2008)*

Adults are becoming increasingly concerned about the values children are learning from those around them. Two thirds of adults think that the moral values of children today are not as strong as when they were children. Children have reported a lack of positive interaction with adults in their communities. 11% of children have complained that adults in their community were 'never' friendly to them and 37% said they were only 'sometimes' friendly. (*The Good Childhood Enquiry, 2008)* The question must then be asked: if children are not receiving affirmation, love, guidance and acceptance from the adults around them then who do they look to as examples?

The media, especially television, plays an important role in the socialization of our children today. In previous generations children received their moral guidance from their schools, families and religious institutions. Today they are bombarded with a toxic mix of sexual imagery influenced by a celebrity culture which is devoid of any moral teaching.

Celebrities are role models for the youth of today. Children imitate their fashion trends and behaviour. Unfortunately some of these so-called role models are not setting good examples. In April 2011, Manchester United footballer Wayne Rooney was given a two-match ban. He had sworn directly into a TV camera, filming live, after scoring a hat-trick. *(BBC Sport, 7 April 2011)* In the media storm that followed it quickly became clear that this behaviour was considered the norm and that many thought Rooney had done nothing wrong.

The promotion of amorality in our culture has the effect of removing all behavioural boundaries. Three young people were found guilty of murdering a young woman with learning difficulties. Two further defendants were found guilty of manslaughter. Gemma Hayter was forced to drink urine, stripped naked, tortured and beaten to death. Some of her attackers were still in their teens. *(Coventry Telegraph, July 2011)*

Society has the responsibility to provide basic moral guidance to its children if it wants to remain viable. Those of a liberal attitude maintain that it is the right of individuals within a civilised society to have freedom of speech, taste and inclination. Yet somewhere along this path to 'liberalisation' we have forgotten the responsibility we have to our young. 'Adult' material is slipping, almost unnoticed and accepted, into the hands of our children.

We have reached the point where the young are being led to conclude that nothing is inherently right or wrong, good or bad, true or false, real or unreal. Nothing is absolute, everything is relative. Therefore, we have the mantra of 'informed choice' and the ridiculous notion of children being encouraged to create their own morality. Eternal verities, passed from one generation to the next, are displaced by situational ethics. This is the pathway to confusion and chaos for the young and to the breakdown of common and cohesive values in society.

Britain today is guilty of shirking its responsibility to its youth and we must all take some part of the blame in this. Politicians needs to re-learn the dictum of William Gladstone: *'Nothing that is morally wrong can be politically right'*.

15 Spiritually Corrupted

- Only 41% of young people believe there is a God. At the same time 35% believe in their daily horoscope, 40% believe in ghosts, 20% believe in black magic and fortune tellers and 31% believe that you can contact the spirit of a dead person. *(Making Sense of Generation Y, 2006)*

- Parents feel encouraging a religious identity at home conflicted with other pressures on their children, including negative portrayals of religion in the media. *(Religion, beliefs & parenting practices, Joseph Rowntree Foundation, 2008)*

- Almost 100,000 pupils are being taught in schools which have dropped Christian assemblies in favour of Islamic or multi-faith worship. *(The Daily Telegraph, 9 January 2010)*

Over many years Britain has embraced people from different faiths and cultures. This is a mark of its Christian foundations which promote freedom of speech and worship. Whereas those of other beliefs are fully embraced, it must be recognised that to accommodate their belief systems will significantly alter the ethos of our society.

There has been a stark move away from traditional Christian belief in our society. Scepticism about religion thrives and God is presented to children in the same way as Father Christmas or the Tooth Fairy. At the same time there has been a movement towards more occult practices and beliefs.

Making Sense of Generation Y, published by the Church of England, shows that young people are claiming to be happy without God. Church attendance is down and *'For every 100 children who were in Sunday School in 1930 there are only 9 today'*. The research in the book seems to suggest that the theory that young people feel they have a 'God shaped hole' within them is a myth. There was little fear of sin or death. Rather than having a feeling of despair and meaninglessness they are finding *'meaning and significance in everyday life, which the popular arts help them to understand'*.

(Making Sense of Generation Y, Church House Publishings, Savage & Collins-Mayo, 2006)

The British Humanist Association *(11 August 2011)* has suggested the use of non-religious events in school assemblies. The anniversaries of famous people's births or deaths, or of historical events, can be used instead of any content with a religious theme. It also makes suggestions to aid schools fulfil any legal obligation they have for a collective act of worship without having to deal with a religious element.

Ofsted *(2010)* inspectors have singled out the study of Christianity as being a source of concern in our schools today. The report stated: *'In many cases, the study of Jesus focused on an unsystematic collection of information about his life, with limited reference to his theological significance within the faith...Insufficient attention was paid to diversity within the Christian tradition and to pupils who were actively engaged in Christian practice...This sometimes contrasted sharply with the more careful attention paid to the experiences of pupils from other religious traditions'.*

Compared with an Ofsted survey three years previously the number of religious education (RE) lessons classified as 'inadequate' in secondary schools has doubled. In many primary schools the quality of RE lessons was 'not good enough'. *(Transforming religious education, Ofsted, June 2010)*

Prominent atheist Richard Dawkins helped set up a summer camp for children who will be taught rational scepticism as well as the other usual camp activities such as canoeing. It will teach that religious beliefs can prevent ethical and moral behaviour. *(The Times, 28 July 2009)*

In February 2008 married couple Eunice and Owen Johns were told they would be unable to foster children anymore. This is despite having a proven track record fostering 15 children and receiving praise from their local authority. Their crime? They have been barred because they are Christians who refused to promote the homosexual lifestyle to small children (aged eight and under) and tell them that the practice of homosexuality is a good thing.

The High Court has said that Christians with traditional views on sexual ethics are unsuitable as foster carers. It said that homosexual 'rights' trump freedom of conscience in the UK. The Judges unreservedly upheld an Equalities and Human Rights Commission (EHRC) submission that children risk being *'infected'* by Christian moral beliefs. This ruling means that thousands of Christians may be barred from fostering, when there is a desperate shortage of foster parents, unless they compromise their beliefs. Many more children will spend their childhoods in children's homes deprived of a family life, love and stability. It is an assault not only on the Christian faith but upon the marriage-based family and denies the importance of a spiritual dimension to children's upbringing and development.

Dr Justin Barrett, a senior researcher at the University of Oxford's Centre for Anthropology and Mind, claims that young people have a predisposition to believe in a supreme being. They have an assumption that everything in the world was created with a purpose, instinctively believing that almost everything has been designed for a particular reason. He says that young children have faith even when they have not been taught about it by family or at school. *"If we threw a handful on an island and they raised themselves I think they would believe in God...Children's normally and naturally developing minds make them prone to believe in divine creation and intelligent design. In contrast, evolution is unnatural for human minds; relatively difficult to believe".* He added that children are more likely to believe in creationism rather than evolution, even if they are told otherwise by parents or teachers. He claims anthropologists have found that in some cultures children believe in God even when religious teachings are withheld from them. *(The Daily Telegraph 24 November 2008)*

Christian influence in the media has been marginalised. Column inches are taken up with mindless chatter about celebrities, star signs and 'alternative' spirituality. The United Kingdom and Western civilisation was built upon Christian teaching and values. Now the only time the name of Jesus is heard in the media is as a curse. Blasphemy is presented as normal and acceptable. Programs like *'Most Haunted'* and *'Psychic Sally'* are ratings winners.

There has been a massive explosion in the number of books based on witchcraft and paganism. An internet search on a well-known online book store reveals, under the search heading of *Books > Horror >*

*Occult > Children's book*s, dozens of books with titles such as '*The Ghost Feeler; Tales of Terror and the Supernatural*', '*The Wicca: and other Tales*' and '*Dreams, Demons and Desire*' alongside more traditional children's books.

There are internet sites that give direction on how to raise your child in the Wicca and pagan faith, series of books you can buy for very young children and even organised holidays for pagan families. Ouija boards are promoted as children's toys - seemingly as harmless as a Monopoly board.

Teenagers are increasingly attracted to the occult with devastating consequences. In 2005 a 14 year old boy, Luke Mitchell, was found guilty of murdering his girlfriend. Luke was obsessed with the 'Goth' culture, obsessed with Marilyn Manson, fantasy horror, drugs and spending time hanging around graveyards. Police found in his room jars of his own urine and a knife pouch with the satanic numbers 666 marked on it. It is not the first time a murder has been associated with such influences. Four years previously a 17 year old boy ritualistically murdered an elderly lady, drinking her blood and admitting to an obsession with vampires. *(TFP Viewpoint, 1 February 2005)*

In British culture secularism is rapidly depriving the young of the spiritual dimension of living and of moral values. This deprivation can be halted only by rejecting the materialism which has created it. The erosion of Christian morality, which is based on love, truth and healing, has led to a spiritual vacuum. This is being filled by less well understood spiritualities, often rooted in death, abuse and hopeless scepticism.

Our children and young people are being presented with the concept of a life without meaning or purpose - a life without inherent value. We are telling our children they have come from nowhere and are going nowhere. This is surely a definition of being lost.

16   The Inevitable Consequences

- 4.7% of children have been raped or forced into sex by another child. *(NSPCC, Child Cruelty in the UK, 2011)*

- 1 in 4 children is bullied. *(Stomp Out Bullying, 2011)*

- A 17-year-old carried out nearly 100 burglaries across Essex and stole several sports cars in a two-year spree worth £445,000. *(UK Police Online, April 2011)*

- 30% of teenagers binge drink weekly. *(Centre of Public Health, 2008)*

In August 2011 the United Kingdom experienced some of the worst rioting it had ever seen. The initial violence, sparked by an incident in London, involved the shooting of a convicted drug dealer by police. Homes, businesses, cars and police stations were burned to the ground. Shops were looted, homes robbed and police attacked. The violence spread to several other cities around the UK. Primarily the perpetrators were teenagers and youths. The reasons given for the rioting were broad and many. Some suggested government cuts, increased immigration and political unease. But when those involved were asked the answer was a resounding *"because I can"* and *"it's fun"*. One of the youngest charged in the riots was an 11 year old girl; others facing charges include a learning mentor, a social work trainee and a law student. *(ITV News, 11 August 2011)*

The truth is we have a lost generation where family breakdown is the norm, instant gratification rules, drugs and alcohol are plentiful, sexual promiscuity flourishes and gang culture has replaced the family. We are reaping the consequences of a rudderless society where we have accepted, appeased and ignored poor and immoral behaviour. There are no longer serious deterrents in society and someone else is always to blame.

Manchester District Judge, Jonathan Feinstein, trying a 14 year old girl charged with looting in the riots, who appeared in court unaccompanied said, *"The parents have to take responsibility for this child. Apart from one case I have not seen any father or mother in court"*.

The National Audit Office (NAO, 2010) estimates young offenders cost the UK economy up to £11bn a year. Although those aged 10-17 years make up only 11% of the population, they are responsible for 17% of crimes committed. Family breakdown, educational under-achievement, substance abuse, mental illness and other problems are all implicated.

"Just over a year ago I was walking past McDonald's in Brixton when scores of teenagers poured out, screaming. A young man had just been shot inside the restaurant in broad daylight...However, in the following months a teenage boy was shot dead inside Streatham Ice Rink. Intruders shot dead a teenage boy at his home in Clapham. And a drive-by shooting, outside a nightclub above Streatham Ice Rink, left a man in his thirties dead. All these victims, like others in similar incidents across south London, were young people with links to violent gangs". *(Steve Reed, MP, February 2008)*

A 14 year old boy has been given one of the toughest ASBOs ever with the added threat of five years in prison if he commits another offence. Since the age of nine he has inflicted chaos in his local area. His crimes include punching other boys and girls, racist abuse and targeting the disabled. He attacked a man who caught him trespassing in his garden, knocking out two of his teeth and terrorised a blind woman by threatening to break her windows. He robbed a boy with special needs, vandalised cars and shops and intimidated witnesses. *(Disability Hate Crime, 1 April 2011)*

In the UK a knife crime happens every 24 minutes. In 2007, 27 teenagers were stabbed to death in London alone. Those at highest risk of knife crime are males aged between 14 and 24. 28% of children in schools say they carry a knife and 3% say they used a knife against another person. *(Say No to Knives, 11 August 2011)* It is clear why so many children are living in fear.

The consequences of poverty in the UK include increased ill health, unemployment and criminal activity. The public service cost of child poverty has been estimated to be somewhere between £10 billion and

£20 billion a year. *(Frank Field Parenting Report, 2011)* The personal cost continues to be measured.

Around 26% (198,000) of babies under the age of one in the UK have parents affected by either one or a combination of the following issues: domestic abuse, substance misuse, mental health problems. 14% of babies (109,000) are living with a parent who is a substance abuser. 19% of babies (144,000) have a parent with a mental health problem. 5% of babies (39,000) have a parent who has experienced domestic abuse in the past year. *(NSPCC, Estimates of the number of infants (under the age of one year) living with substance misusing parents, 2011)*

We invite into our homes, and even children's bedrooms, sights, sounds and experiences that worry, confuse, intimidate and frighten children and young people: *"I am very upset. This man on the internet has got me to do things on the webcam before by threatening me that he would tell my friends about what I do. I changed my internet identity but he found me again and forced me to do things again. I don't want to tell the police". (Girl, aged 18) (Childline Case notes on sexual abuse, November 2009) "I was chatting to a boy who is 15 years old on the MSN this evening. He flashed his private parts to me via webcam. I am scared and worried". (Girl, aged nine) (Childline Case notes on sexual abuse, November 2009)*

What we invite into our homes influences our children in other ways. An 8 year old boy killed himself shortly after watching a film that features ritualistic suicides. Lewis McGlynn was found hanged after watching *'The Last Samurai'*. The film has a 15 certificate. Lewis had a large number of DVDs in his bedroom belonging to his older brother. His parents did not stop him watching them. He had a habit of playing out scenes in films. The 2003 film contains gory samurai customs including seppuku, a suicide ritual by disembowelment. In one scene a man stabs himself in the stomach with a knife before he is beheaded by another man. *(Daily Mail, 11 August 2011)*

Bullying remains a major issue in our schools today but is drastically different from the bullying faced by children in previous generations.

With almost 40% of children experiencing feelings of fear about going to school because of bullying the cost cannot be underestimated.

(Herefordshire Council, 2011) The long term effects of bullying include depression, low self esteem, self harm and even suicide. *Beatbullying (2010)* suggests that 44% of suicides in children age 11-14 may be related to bullying.

Almost every child in the UK has access to social networking sites through the internet or mobile phones. 'Cyber bullying' can be very damaging to children, leading to anxiety, depression and even suicide. Over half of children have been bullied online. Shockingly around 50% have also taken part in cyber bullying. Over a third have experienced cyber threats online and over a quarter have been bullied via their mobiles or the internet. *(Bully Statistics, 11 August 2011)*

Nine teenagers were charged over the death of a 15 year old girl who killed herself after months of merciless and violent bullying by fellow pupils at an American school. Phoebe Prince took her life after being tormented both physically and online. Charges include criminal harassment, stalking and breach of civil rights through text messages and abuse on Facebook. This case follows several others where children have killed themselves following cyber bullying. *(The Guardian, 30 March 2010)*

Children as young as five are being excluded for sexual misconduct in our schools. Young Voice *(2008)* found that children are not only being forced to do something sexual but are also being forced to watch. In the school year 2007/8 there were 3,450 fixed period exclusions and 120 expulsions from schools in England due to sexual misconduct. This includes incidents such as groping and using sexually insulting language. *(Department for Children, Schools and Families, 2009)*

One in three children at primary school in England is overweight. *(BBC News, January 2011).* There are an estimated 22 million overweight or obese children in the world today. *(Patient, 2011)* Obesity during childhood is a health concern in itself, but can also lead to physical and mental health problems in later life, such as heart disease, diabetes, osteoarthritis, back pain, increased risk of cancer, low self-esteem and depression. *(ISD Scotland, December 2009)*

The reasons for obesity in childhood are as complex as they are simple. Lack of exercise, too much screen time and bad diet are major factors. Parents often deny the problem in their child, attributing extra weight to 'puppy fat'. Children find that eating replaces the comfort missing in their lives and self-soothe with food. (*BUPA health fact sheet*)

Even more worrying is the increase in eating disorders in children. In a three year period over 2,000 children received NHS treatment for eating disorders. Nearly 600 children under the age of 13 years were treated in hospital in England, 197 were aged between 5 and 9 years and 98 were aged between 5 and 7 years at the time of treatment. Approximately 400 were between the ages of 10 and 12 and more than 1,500 between 13 and 15 years. One in three hospital admissions for eating disorders involved a child. (*The Guardian, 1 August 2011*)

Pro-ana (promoting anorexia), pro-mia (promoting bulimia) and pro-suicide sites are easily available for viewing on the internet. These sites teach, instruct and give guidance on how to make these 'life-style' choices successfully. These sites are degrading children's mental health by facilitating access to information that children would not normally have access to. (*University of New Hampshire, 2012*)

Binge drinking has become a major curse. Natasha Farnham (14 years) was taken to hospital after drinking 16 bottles of wine, cider and spirits in a three-day period. Diagnosed with liver failure, usually suffered by middle-aged alcoholics, she was told to stop drinking. She stopped attending school and stole to buy alcohol. Doctors told her she will die if she drinks again. She now also has memory loss. *"I didn't think my drinking was a problem because all my friends were getting wasted as well...I suppose I thought I looked grown-up and would drink as much as possible - sometimes even passing out...But now I have no short term memory and doctors warn me that if I drink any more I will die"*. (*The Daily Telegraph, 15 April 2011*) This story is not unique. Children are drinking themselves into oblivion as a way to deal with the pain and hopelessness of the real world.

17 The Cry of Our Children

- One in four women in prison has spent time in local authority care as a child. *(Women in Prison, 21 July 2011)*

- There are 83,000 looked-after children in the UK. *(Barnardo's, 9 August 2011)*

- Every day, on average, eight children and young people talk to ChildLine specifically about suicide. *(Childline case notes on suicide, 2009)*

- One in eight young people had been physically hurt and one in nine sexually assaulted when they ran away from home. *(Biehal N et al. Lost from view: missing persons in the UK. 2003. Research Summary, Social Work Research and Development Unit, University of York)*

- 34% of children and young people say they are always worried about something. A significant number - 11% - are extremely worried. *(NSPCC, 2004)*

In 2007/08, ChildLine counselled 2,925 children and young people about suicide. Children and young people told ChildLine that their concerns were not taken seriously by parents or by health professionals. *(Childline Case notes on suicide, 2009)*

One suicidal child told a counsellor *"I hug myself and pretend someone else is comforting me"*. That a child feels so alone that death is their only friend is a damning reflection of the society we live in. *(Childline, 2011)*

We are told by society that the need for fathers is greatly diminished today. Yet, when asked, children clearly tell us they not only need a father but that they want one too. Findings show that young people's relationships both with their fathers and with their mothers are linked to their well-being and self-esteem. *(Fatherhood Commission, The Children's Society, 11 August 2011)*

Experts blame the breakdown of family life for the rise of gang culture. The gang has replaced the family unit and provides youngsters with a structure and a sense of belonging which generates the *'post code pride'* which can lead to murder. *(The British Library, 11 August 2011)* Our children are telling us they need more from the adults in their lives.

The behaviour of children today has been widely criticised but should be recognised as evidence of the failure of adult society to provide for their real needs.

Vast numbers of children run away from home each year and it is estimated that in the UK this number totals 100,000. 11% of all children in the UK run away from home or are forced to leave. 80% of 16 year olds who run away say it is because of 'problems at home' with 12% of young people saying the experience or the threat of physical abuse or violence, emotional abuse or emotional neglect, domestic violence, sexual abuse or being scared was the reason they ran away. 10% of those who run away had done so before their 11th birthday and 68% of young people who have run away overnight said they had not been reported by their parents or carers as missing to the police. *(The Children's Society, Still Running II, 2005)*

10% of young people say they hate leaving home in the morning because of problems at school yet 5% of young people say they hate coming back from school because of problems at home. *(NSPCC, 2004)*

A quarter of the 1,600 children held in young offenders' institutions in England and Wales have been in care. Reoffending rates are high among youth offenders. *(The Ministry of Justice, 2011)*

Many children are living in constant fear. A survey by the *Journal of Counselling and Development* of children aged 7-18 years found that some of the fears they experience daily were terrorist attacks, having to fight in a war, drive-by shootings, tornadoes/hurricanes and drowning. The top five fears of a seven year old were *'1.Being kidnapped 2. Myself dying 3. AIDS 4. Not being able to breathe 5. Being threatened with a gun'. (CNN, April 2009)*

The fastest rate of increase in depression is among young people. Causes of teen and childhood depression include social rejection, family problems and exam pressure. Prescriptions for anti-depressants and other mind-altering drugs made out to children under 16 years have more than quadrupled in the last decade. There were more than 631,000 prescribed to children under 16 years in the 2006-2007 financial year. This is compared to just 146,000 in 1996/97. *(The Guardian, July 2007)*

One NHS Trust had 324 referrals of young people suffering from depression between September 2010 and August 2011. A further 378 patients were referred for other mental health therapies. Some of the children were as young as five. *(NHS Solent, 2012)*

Along with depression, the risk of self-harm in young people is increasing. It is used as a way of dealing with very complicated feelings. Young people do it because they have been feeling desperate about a problem and do not know where to turn for help, they feel trapped and helpless, want to relieve stress, cope with feelings of shame, to punish themselves; self-injury helps them to feel more in control. Some do it to feel more connected and alive and some even with the intent to die. *(Self-harm, suicide and risk: helping people who self-harm. The Royal College of Psychiatrists, College Report CR158 June 2010)*

Children and young people are finding it harder and harder to cope with the pressures of modern life. The stress they are under must no longer be ignored by society.

Enormous numbers of children are experiencing abuse, assault, persecution and neglect. Many feel they have nowhere to turn and no one with whom they can share their problems. They are lonely, hurting and desperate for help. They are the product of the selfish, materialistic society we have created.

The voices of multitudes of children cry out for the love and care that a civilised and caring society should surely be providing.

18   Our Legacy to Our Children

- The UK population is projected to increase to 67.2 million by 2020 and to 73.2 million in 2035. *(Office for National Statistics 23 November 2011)*

- At least £17 billion of extra tax rises or spending cuts will be needed in 2017 to get Britain's debt back to pre-crisis levels by 2061. *(The Office for Budget Responsibility 12 July 2012)*

- Household debt has risen in every quarter since the start of 2011 and is expected to jump by a further 26%, from £1.58 trillion to £2 trillion, between now and the end of 2016. *(Daily Telegraph 27 August 2012)*

The UK population is projected to continue ageing with the average age rising from 39.7 years in 2010 to 39.9 years in 2020 and 42.2 years by 2035. Under current legislation, the number of people of state pension age is projected to increase by 28% from 12.2 million to 15.6 million by 2035. *(Office for National Statistics 26 October 2011)*

Professor Niall Ferguson entitled the first of his 2012 Reith Lectures 'We're mortgaging the future of the younger generation'. He said *'the heart of the matter is the way public debt allows the current generation of voters to live at the expense of those as yet too young to vote or as yet unborn'.*

A 50% increase in the number of people over the age of 65 is forecast - 12.9 million by 2030. With the rest of Europe, the UK faces an increasingly aged population with a decreasing workforce to support them. Today there are 5.3 people of working age to help pay for every citizen who is 70-plus. By 2030 that will have dropped to 3.7. *(Daily Telegraph 27 August 2012)*

With 938,000 of 16-24 year olds not in education, employment or training *(Department for Education, 2011)* the future is bleak for our young people. They have little to look forward to and few goals to motivate them.

In 2010 the average debt for a student leaving university was £17,500. This is now considerably greater and destined to increase with the additional burden of raised tuition fees. Many have failed to find work and are claiming benefits.

Many more are leaving school with no meaningful qualification. There is little hope of this situation changing in the foreseeable future. This is demoralizing and depressing for our young. Heavy debts, poor pay and lack of opportunity are stalling their walk into adult life: *"if an entire generation of people are growing up to find they have no access to jobs and homes with which they will build their adult lives it's not a big surprise, surely, that they fail to 'take responsibility'"*. *(Jilted Generation, Howker & Malik, 2010)*

The greed of the current adult generation has created a huge burden of debt which will be foisted on the next generation.

Our failure to invest in the lives of our children in the UK is leaving them with not only a negative financial inheritance but, more importantly, an uncertainty about personal identity and purpose.

The undermining of the secure Judaeo-Christian foundations upon which Britain was built now leaves future generations building their lives on shifting sand. Do we really wish to see these foundations destroyed? If so, are we prepared to accept the dire consequences of this for future generations? If not, what are we prepared to do to strengthen them?

19 Jesus and Children

Each one of us is made in God's image. Every person, child or adult, is of immense value and is known and loved personally by God. He knew us in our mother's womb. He calls us by our name and even the hairs on our head are numbered. These truths are the basis of our Christian civilisation in which every individual has basic rights and responsibilities.

Children are especially precious. They are a gift from God *(see Psalm 127 v3)*. They are entrusted to us by God and we have a clear responsibility for them.

Jesus loves children and declares that when we receive a child we receive Him.

'He took a little child whom he placed among them. Taking the child in his arms, he said to them, "Whoever welcomes one of these little children in my name welcomes me; and whoever welcomes me does not welcome me but the one who sent me."' (Mark 9.36-37)

Jesus reaches out to bless children.

'Jesus said, "Let the little children come to me, and do not hinder them, for the kingdom of heaven belongs to such as these." When he had placed his hands on them, he went on from there.' (Matthew 19.14-15)

Jesus gives a fierce warning which rings loud and clear today.

"If anyone causes one of these little ones—those who believe in me— to stumble, it would be better for them to have a large millstone hung around their neck and to be drowned in the depths of the sea. Woe to the world because of the things that cause people to stumble! Such things must come, but woe to the person through whom they come!" (Matthew 18.5-7)

This is the measure of the seriousness with which God, our Father, regards the way in which we treat our children.

Jesus is full of love and compassion. He wants us to love children with the same compassion. Just as Jesus expressed His love in both tears and anger, so today we should weep and be angry in the face of what is being done to our children.

The Christian Gospel is hope-filled and is about the healing of all relationships - for individuals, for families, for society and for the world. The way of Jesus gives hope to children everywhere.

20 What on Earth can We do?

The evidence presented in this book is irrefutable and very disturbing.

The terrible situations facing vast numbers of children are extremely serious. Many, on reading this information, will inevitably feel overwhelmed and helpless, whilst others may feel despondent and depressed.

Amongst children and young people themselves there is widespread disillusionment and despair, especially in the UK.

The first necessary response is to believe that we can make a difference, however small that difference may seem. No-one can do everything but everyone can do something. Everyone has a role to play. The worst response is to believe that this is a problem for someone else to solve.

How do we discover what we can do?

- **Firstly:** we can *listen* to what children and young people are saying. Whether through the children near to us or the children reported in this book, we need to face the facts about what is happening to children.

- **Secondly:** we can *express* our sorrow and guilt for what we have individually and collectively done and failed to do. We need to repent.

- **Thirdly:** we can *commit* ourselves to action. This could be to speak out and challenge the influences which are damaging and harming children and young people across the world. It could also be to find out about ways to become more involved in work for children.

There are many charities and organisations working in a huge variety of ways for the good of children and young people. The Maranatha Community is in close touch with many of these and will be pleased to give further information on request.

"All that is necessary for the triumph of evil is that good men do nothing". Edmund Burke

Another Portrait

Stacey had a tough start in life as her relationship with her family broke down and she was put into 'care' at the age of 11 years. She left school without qualifications but managed to find work and started to settle down with her boyfriend.

Everything collapsed when her boyfriend introduced her to heroin. It took over her life and she turned to shop-lifting and burglary to fund her habit. She was fired from her job and eventually was caught and sentenced to prison.

Stacey spent 9 years in prison on 5 separate convictions. She described it as like being in a revolving door – in and out of prison. She had no support and every time she resolved to stay off heroin she failed.

During her last prison sentence she became a Christian through a team working in the prison. She says, *"I discovered the unconditional love and acceptance I needed. The closer I got to God, the more I changed. He filled that hole I'd been looking to fill for years, using drugs, trying to impress people. I finally knew that I was fully wanted."*

Stacey went on to realise that prison could work for her good – she did lots of courses with the support of the visiting Christian team, which gave her the strength to deal with life after she was released. They helped her to get a job, a flat and a local church.

Stacey says, *"I was released as a Priority and Prolific Offender (PPO) because of my past. It means they watch you much more closely. But my probation officer was so impressed with my new attitude I was released from the scheme within 7 months, which at the time was the quickest on record."*

"I look back now and think: who was that person? I can safely say if I hadn't met the team and become a Christian, I'd have been in and out of prison for the rest of my life."

Taken from '20 Celebrating Two Decades of Changed Lives' with the kind permission of The Message Trust, 2011

The Innocents

They come as gift
beyond all price
small, weak
defenceless and alone.

They come
each known and named
and loved by You.

They come,
each special,
into the place of safety
to be nurtured, protected
and prepared
for the next stage
of their journey
when, though separate
they still remain
dependent, vulnerable,
crying out for care
support and love.

You, who made them
entrust them
to us in all
our human frailty
placing them
directly into our hands.

You hold us accountable
for each precious life,
responsible for these
Your little ones
made carefully, in Your image,
reflecting Your beauty
Your divinity, Your glory.
And in their coming
into our midst
they feel and know
the warmth or coldness
of our welcome,

the peace or tension
of our response,
embracing the joy and love
and tenderness
or repelled by the strange
chilling insecurity,
rejection and neglect.

And in those
early days and years
a high drama
is being
played out.
The imprinted
images and sounds
and words
will remain, deeply held
in memory over all
the coming years,
the happiness, the pain
the trauma and delight.

And we -
are we aware
of the blessings we can give
and injuries inflict?
Do we see
the fierce battle
which soon rages
for the heart
and mind and soul
of each of these
Your little ones?
Are we blind
to the dark wild jungle
through which
they will walk,
surrounding them,
ever ready

to corrupt, abuse,
exploit, consume?
Do we know
the seeds now sown
in fertile minds and hearts
will bring forth fruits
of blessing or destruction?
Do we care
that the marks
now being imprinted
in the soft clay
of innocent lives
may in truth
be the vicious wounds
of a cruel, godless world
inflicted before
our very eyes?
Is it nothing to us
that soon or late
a wild, ferocious harvest
will be reaped
and that
its agony, violence,
corruption and rottenness
will be placed at our door?
- attributed to us?
Do we imagine
that we will not
be held responsible
for the trail
of misery and suffering

of the innocents?
Can we deceive ourselves
that a loving God
stands by uncaring?
Can we turn away
from the truth
that ultimately,
inevitably
we will each have
to give account
of ourselves
and each face
the judgement of
almighty God?

And then the question
will surely be put:
'Why
as I came to you
in these
my little ones,
crying out
for food
and nourishment,
why
did you feed me
poison?
Why?'

Dennis Wrigley

"Finally...
whatever is true,
whatever is honourable,
whatever is just,
whatever is pure,
whatever is lovely,
whatever is commendable,
if there is any excellence,
if there is anything worthy of praise,
think about these things."
(Philippians 4.8 ESV)